ISSUE 2, FEBRUARY 2018

AUSTRALIAN FOREIGN AFFAIRS

Contributors 2

Editor's Note 3

Michael Wesley
The Pivot to Chaos 7

Kim Beazley and L. Gordon Flake
North Korea's Missile Stand-off 27

Andrew Davies
Can Australia Fight Alone? 43

David Kilcullen
Letter from Washington 67

Reviews
Anna Fifield *Asia's Reckoning* by Richard McGregor 85
Cynthia Banham *Incorrigible Optimist* by Gareth Evans 89
Jonathan Head *Blood and Silk* by Michael Vatikiotis 93
Mary-Louise O'Callaghan *Australia's Northern Shield?* by Bruce Hunt 97
Ian Verrender *Straight Talk on Trade* by Dani Rodrik 101
Hamish McDonald *The Army and the Indonesian Genocide*
by Jess Melvin 104

Correspondence
"Mugged by Sentiment": Rory Medcalf, Richard Menhinick,
James Curran 109
"The Changing Face of Australia": Jieh-Yung Lo, John Fitzgerald 116

The Back Page by Richard Cooke 128

Contributors

Cynthia Banham is a visitor at the Australian National University and a University of Queensland research fellow.

Kim Beazley is a former defence minister and former Australian ambassador to the United States.

Andrew Davies is a program director at the Australian Strategic Policy Institute.

Anna Fifield is the Tokyo bureau chief for the *Washington Post*.

L. Gordon Flake is the CEO of Perth USAsia Centre.

Jonathan Head is the BBC South-East Asia correspondent.

David Kilcullen is a US-based counterterrorism expert, a former Australian Army officer and a contributing editor at the *Australian*.

Hamish McDonald is world editor of the *Saturday Paper* and the author of two books about Indonesia.

Mary-Louise O'Callaghan is a former South Pacific correspondent for Fairfax Media and the *Australian*.

Ian Verrender is the ABC's business editor.

Michael Wesley is dean of the College of Asia and the Pacific at the Australian National University.

Australian Foreign Affairs is published three times a year by Schwartz Publishing Pty Ltd. Publisher: Morry Schwartz. ISBN 978-1-76064-0293 ISSN 2208-5912 ALL RIGHTS RESERVED. No part of this publication may be reproduced, stored in a retrieval system, or transmitted in any form by any means electronic, mechanical, photocopying, recording or otherwise without the prior consent of the publishers. Essays, reviews and correspondence © retained by the authors. Subscriptions – 1 year print & digital auto-renew (3 issues): $49.99 within Australia incl. GST. 1 year print and digital subscription (3 issues): $59.99 within Australia incl. GST. 2 years print & digital (6 issues): $114.99 within Australia incl. GST. 1 year digital only: $29.99. Payment may be made by MasterCard, Visa or Amex, or by cheque made out to Schwartz Publishing Pty Ltd. Payment includes postage and handling. To subscribe, fill out and post the subscription card or form inside this issue, or subscribe online: www.australianforeignaffairs. com or subscribe@australianforeignaffairs.com Phone: 1800 077 514 or 61 3 9486 0288. Correspondence should be addressed to: The Editor, Australian Foreign Affairs Level 1, 221 Drummond Street Carlton VIC 3053 Australia Phone: 61 3 9486 0288 / Fax: 61 3 9486 0244 Email: enquiries@australianforeignaffairs.com Editor: Jonathan Pearlman. Associate Editor: Chris Feik. Consulting Editor: Allan Gyngell. Deputy Editors: Kirstie Innes-Will and Julia Carlomagno. Management: Caitlin Yates. Marketing: Elisabeth Young and Georgia Mill. Publicity: Anna Lensky. Design: Peter Long. Production Coordinator: Hanako Smith. Typesetting: Tristan Main. Cover image by T.J. Kirkpatrick / Bloomberg via Getty Images. Printed in Australia by McPherson's Printing Group.

TRUMP IN ASIA

onald Trump's election victory was described by some of his more anguished critics as an "American tragedy," but this vastly understates the extent of the problem.

The tragedy – and any fallout – is global.

Trump's leadership, marred as it is by a mix of inwardness, ignorance, lies, vanity and incoherence, is undermining the credibility, power and prestige of a nation that remains the world's dominant military, economic and cultural power. Despite the phenomenal rise of China, it is worth recounting the ways in which the United States continues to lead in each of these spheres. Its military spending last year was more than triple that of China (which ranked second); the US dollar remains the world's chief reserve currency, and America's gross domestic product was 50 per cent higher than China's (which ranked second); and the website, film and television show with the largest global reach in 2017 were, respectively, Google, *Star Wars: The Last Jedi* and *Game of Thrones*.

The United States' grip on power is weakening, particularly in Asia, but it starts from an extraordinarily high base. Which is to say: Trump not only has much to lose, but also a capacity to cause immeasurable global harm. International agreements on climate change and trade are scrapped or in doubt; tensions in North Korea edge closer to war, possibly nuclear; and everywhere, xenophobes and demagogues are emboldened.

For Australia, this poses two main challenges.

The first is to conduct and develop the relationship with the country's main ally when it is led by a president whose personality is tempestuous and whose instinct is to mistrust alliances.

The second involves responding to the impact that Trump will have on a fast-changing Asia. China ranks second on most global indices of power but it is catching up, fast. Its economy's size, adjusted for price differences, already exceeds that of the United States. Militarily, most analysts believe that, in a war in its neighbourhood, such as over Taiwan, some of its capabilities could match those of the US. There is little sign – despite Trump's claim after his twelve-day trip to Asia – of a "great American comeback."

The power balance in Asia is changing, Trump fuels the instability, and countries are reacting. Australia and Japan are forging closer defence ties, with the prospect of Japanese troops returning to Darwin. The two nations are considering more formal arrangements with India and the US – an embrace viewed unhappily by China. Australia and others in the region are re-examining old enmities and considering new alignments, as well as the type of defences they require and the associated cost, as they try to understand their place in this rapidly evolving global order.

Jonathan Pearlman

THE PIVOT TO CHAOS

Australia, Asia
and the president
without a plan

Michael Wesley

No American president – indeed, no modern celebrity – has so monop-olised our attention as Donald Trump. Rarely is the T-word far from the centre of conversation and consciousness; it's a trigger for humour, outrage, despair and mystification. A dollop of the Donald brings effervescence to any discussion. Trump has become the harbinger of so much that alarms us in our contemporary world: populism, politi-cal polarisation, crass consumerism, middle-class despair, the decay of respect and moral standards.

Except in Asia. Obsession with Trump is a Western phenomenon. Of course, the forty-fifth American president is discussed in Asian soci-eties, but not with the same intensity as in the West. To travel to Asia is to enter – blissfully – a Trump-muted zone, free from the satura-tion coverage of every tweet and micro-detail in the White House soap opera. The American president is spoken about, but in a business-like, unemotional way – and then the conversation moves on. Talking about US foreign policy in Jakarta, New Delhi or Manila reminds one of what such discussion was like in our society before Trump was elected.

And yet the impact of Trump will arguably be greater in Asia than in any other region. Asia has relied heavily on American power, rather than on institutions and rules, to provide the stability that has allowed the region's astonishingly rapid development. It is also where a rising China represents the most determined and sustainable challenge to American power. Asian states are not blind to the sudden change of direction in American foreign policy delivered by the Trump administration. They simply view American power differently to us. Understanding this difference will be essential to how Australia adjusts its relations with its region during the Trump era.

America's triumph

To comprehend the magnitude of Trump's impact on the United States' role in Asia, we need to begin with the past quarter-century of bipartisan American strategy in the region. American foreign policy focused on a single objective after the Cold War: to prevent the rise of a rival power similar to the Soviet Union. There were three elements to this strategy.

First, the United States would preserve the alliances and security partnerships that had been developed to ward off the Soviet threat, even if the threat had ended. These alliances would become the anchors of American primacy – ensuring the US had willing supporters as well as military access to bases and ports around the region – and the guarantees of a stable, predictable international order. In the absence of the original threat to Washington's alliances, American diplomacy worked quietly to build an alternative rationale. America's allies would help defend and extend an open, rules-based and institutionally rich community of states. It was a shift to which most American allies (NATO, Japan, South Korea and Australia, but notably not Thailand and the Philippines) readily agreed. So it was that a decade after the end of the Cold War, America's European and Pacific allies found themselves fighting side by side in Afghanistan and Iraq. This globe-spanning coalition – with the US at the helm – was a working model of the new world order.

The second prong of US post–Cold War strategy was to strengthen and broaden regional and global institutions, welcoming in former or prospective rivals as partners, as a way of convincing any challengers to join and abide by the rules of the American-led international order. The more states that adhered to the prevailing rules, the harder and more costly it would be for any country, no matter how powerful, to flout them. So China and, later, Russia were welcomed into the Asia-Pacific Economic Cooperation (APEC) forum and the World Trade Organization (WTO). American strategists believed that the quickening globalisation of the world economy would deliver significant development gains to former or prospective rivals, thereby removing any incentive to buck the system or try to change it.

Third, the United States would maintain peace through strength, by extending its power in such a way that any potential challenger would conclude that competing with it was futile. The 1991 war against Saddam Hussein had demonstrated the American military edge in stark terms: precision-guided missiles, ballistic missile defence systems, electronic warfare capabilities, space-based surveillance and control, networked combat communications. The United States could dispatch opponents clinically and emphatically, blinding their defences, surgically destroying their fighting capabilities and eliminating their ability to mount a further challenge. Faced with such a fate, and a hyperpower accelerating its research and development of these capabilities, any rational rival would surely simply accede to the unipolar order.

These were global objectives, but they applied especially in the Asia-Pacific. Japan, South Korea and Australia each accepted a renegotiation of the bases of their alliances with the United States, with Tokyo embarking on the slow and emotionally fraught process of changing its pacifist constitution to allow its armed forces to support American military action much further from its home islands. In Thailand and the Philippines, post-colonial sensitivities about foreign bases saw US troops quietly withdraw once the Cold War threat had receded; but America acquired new partners in the region, such as Singapore. Washington encouraged its allies and partners in the Pacific to cooperate with one another, giving rise to an increasingly crowded schedule of joint training and military exercises.

Meanwhile, institution-building became a growth industry in the Asia-Pacific. APEC, the ASEAN Regional Forum (ARF), the Asia–Europe meeting (ASEM) and the East Asia Summit (EAS) – replete with their awkwardly contrived group photo sessions – were the result. China was initially reluctant to join any regional body; famously, it took the sort of cajoling that only foreign minister Gareth Evans could deploy to drag Beijing into the ARF. Other outsiders to the regional order, such as Vietnam, Cambodia, Laos and Myanmar, were also welcomed in.

American firepower was again on display throughout the 1990s and 2000s, in the Balkans, Afghanistan and Iraq. So confident had the Pentagon become in its technical capabilities, it decided that Saddam Hussein could be dispatched with a fraction of the soldiers deployed in round one.

Where Australia and the NATO allies differed from America's Asian allies was in the meaning they ascribed to American power

US power was less visible in Asia than in Europe. Other than American bases in Japan and South Korea, there were no day-to-day reminders of the American security guarantee as there were in Europe and the Persian Gulf. And yet US pre-eminence was an accepted fact in Asia, allowing development and prosperity to deepen and spread in the trans-millennial decades.

Where Australia and the NATO allies differed from America's Asian allies was in the meaning they ascribed to American power.

The Western allies of the United States interpreted American might in moral terms: as the natural outcome of the evolution of history towards democracy, the rule of law, free markets, cosmopolitan equality and the globalised concord of nations. American power, as the ultimate expression of irreversible human progress, was assumed to be unassailable and unchallengeable. It was the moral interpretation of American power that provoked such outrage when that power was seen to be misused during the invasion of Iraq in 2003.

Beyond its Muslim-majority countries, no such outrage occurred in Asia, because in this region, power is generally regarded in much more matter-of-fact, material terms. Asian societies' long memories of the rise and fall of empires, and cycles of subjugation and conquest, dispose them to view power more dispassionately. Despite cultural traditions that hold to a belief in divinely sanctioned rule, Asian societies tend to view power beyond their borders as an inevitable occurrence, to be harnessed, resisted or avoided as the circumstances dictate. Singapore's former prime minister Goh Chok Tong exhibited this attitude when he talked about US power at the start of this century:

> There is a grudging acceptance that the US continues to be a stabilising factor in the region. While there are differences in how each ASEAN country sees the US security presence, there is an underlying recognition that without it, the politics of the region would be more complex and troublesome.

The shock of the Donald

The Trump administration has decisively broken with the bipartisan approach that has guided two Republican and two Democratic presidents since the end of the Cold War. Trump sees American alliances and security partnerships not in terms of threats or promotion of a world order, but as direct cost–benefit equations. The president's default setting is to view allies as freeloaders that exploit US generosity and naivety for their own benefit. Warnings to allies to pay their fair share, thought bubbles about Japan and South Korea acquiring nuclear deterrents, and telephone tantrums about bad deals on asylum seekers take the concept of alliances back to the eighteenth century: as temporary alignments of convenience, easily disposable as the circumstances dictate. Trump's behaviour towards his allies is a stark reminder of just how profoundly his predecessors, stretching back to Harry Truman, had revolutionised the concept of alliances into enduring expressions of values and co-investment in global order.

The president's default setting is to view allies as freeloaders that exploit US generosity

Nor does Trump see global or regional institutions as anything other than bad deals needing renegotiation. Last September, he told the United Nations, a body that encapsulates Roosevelt's vision of an American-led liberal world order:

The United States will forever be a great friend to the world, and especially to its allies. But we can no longer be taken advantage of, or enter into a one-sided deal where the United States gets nothing in return ... While America will pursue cooperation and commerce with other nations, we are renewing our commitment to the first duty of every government: the duty of our citizens.

And in November he harangued APEC leaders in these terms:

We can no longer tolerate these chronic trade abuses, and we will not tolerate them. Despite years of broken promises, we were told that someday soon everyone would behave fairly and responsibly. People in America and throughout the Indo-Pacific region have waited for that day to come. But it never has, and that is why I am here today – to speak frankly about our challenges and work toward a brighter future for all of us.

In the midst of an institution dedicated to regional dialogue, collective benefits and general reciprocity, Trump invited APEC members to negotiate bilateral trade deals with the United States. To date, none has taken up his offer.

But perhaps the most profound break with the traditions of American statecraft is Trump's deep antipathy to the notion that the United States needs to state clear and consistent principles that will guide its foreign policy. Until now, it has been standard practice for presidents to enunciate a "doctrine," thereby providing America's friends and rivals with a clear and dependable framework for understanding how Washington may react to events and proposals. Bush senior spruiked a "new world order"; Clinton spoke of enlarging the community of democracies and free markets; Bush junior, of enforcing order; Obama outlined a "pivot" to Asia. But for Trump, the great dealmaker, having a strategy is bad strategy. A clearly enunciated doctrine makes the United States predictable and exploitable; keeping your counterparts guessing is the key to getting the best deal. Unpredictability is as central to this president's approach to international affairs as resolve and clarity were to his predecessors.

A rival rises

For Western publics, so profound a break with America's animating principles upsets their moral understanding of international power and its purpose. Not only has American power become deeply suspect in the hands of an unpredictable president, but suddenly the longevity of the United States' role as the world's pre-eminent power has become doubtful. The international community's acquiescence to Trump-style American leadership can't be taken for granted. Trump presents a vision of American power with no legitimating purpose beyond advancing specific US interests. As last December's National Security Strategy put it, "a world that supports American interests and reflects our values makes America more secure and prosperous. We will compete and lead in multilateral organisations so that

America's interests and principles are protected." Rather than US power serving global order, now global order must serve US power.

There is no such hand-wringing in Asian societies. Sure, they're disconcerted. Blood pressure has skyrocketed in protocol departments across the Western Pacific. But no one is commissioning White Papers or root-and-branch reviews of what Trump means for the region's future. Asian governments seem determined to keep calm and carry on.

Part of the reason is that the relative decline of American power has been obvious for the best part of a decade in Asia. By 2008 there was little doubt that the United States' strategy for preventing the rise of a new rival in China had not worked in this region. The policy of converting alliances and security partnerships in the Pacific into order-buttressing institutions had been successful. But their attention had been focused either on global concerns, such as preventing the spread of nuclear weapons through the Proliferation Security Initiative, or beyond the region, in fighting militant Islamism in Central Asia and the Middle East. The regional institutions that were intended to socialise rivals to the rules of the game had a fatal design flaw: all were based on the ASEAN principle of consensus, depriving them of the ability to sanction bad behaviour or even to discuss contentious issues. And the serial demonstrations of American military prowess didn't deter rivals; they motivated them to compete with and try to neutralise the United States' cutting-edge technologies.

China understood America's post–Cold War strategy but never acceded to it. Initially it read the collapse of the Soviet Union as the catastrophic consequence of directly opposing the United States and boycotting the globalising world economy. For Deng Xiaoping, it was axiomatic that China should make the most of the US-led order to develop and build its strength, even at the cost of temporarily complying with its prevailing rules. Deng's formula became a guiding mantra: "Observe calmly, secure our position, cope with affairs calmly, hide our capacities and bide our time, be good at maintaining a low profile, and never claim leadership." In 1996 Beijing retreated when President Clinton sent two aircraft-carrier battle groups to the Taiwan Strait after China

Rather than US power serving global order, now global order must serve US power

began military exercises to dissuade the Taiwanese from endorsing a pro-independence president. It accepted Washington's stringent conditions as the price of joining the WTO.

But as China continued to grow in wealth and power, Deng's dictum became harder to stomach. A turning point came in April 2001, when a Chinese jet fighter collided with an American EP-3 surveillance aircraft near the Chinese island of Hainan. The collision was the result of rising Chinese anger at US surveillance activities around its maritime borders, and its increasingly belligerent pushback against these activities. Beijing's refusal to release the plane and its crew until

Washington apologised signalled a new assertiveness in dealing with the sole superpower.

From this point onwards, the logic of Beijing's deepening rivalry with the United States became self-reinforcing. China became more forthright as it grew increasingly dissatisfied with its geopolitical circumstances, which saw it unable to claim sovereignty over Taiwan, and penned in by an island chain dominated by Washington and its allies. Continued acceptance of US primacy meant that Beijing could never alter this situation. The more powerful China became, the more urgent its prerogatives seemed, and the more problematic American supremacy appeared.

China's challenge to the American-led order in the Asia-Pacific occurred in three forms. First, as Beijing realised that regional institutions couldn't sanction its behaviour, it began to take a much more active role within them. China found that it could use its economic power to make friends within ASEAN, creating crucial blocking votes against any issues that could embarrass it. Meanwhile, these regional institutions became forums in which China could stress the peaceful nature of its rise. Rather than being platforms for socialising China into the regional order, Asia-Pacific organisations became mechanisms that Beijing could use to accustom the region to China's power and preferences. By early this decade, China had begun to go beyond existing institutions, proposing its own regional development banks and funds and the Belt and Road infrastructure initiative as new forms of China-centered regional integration. The era has arrived in which China is the institutional entrepreneur in this part of the world.

Second, China began to challenge the American lead in military power. The regular displays of American military prowess alarmed the Chinese Communist Party. China began investing heavily in advanced military technologies: hypersonic, precision-guided missiles; submarines and anti-submarine warfare; space-based weapons systems; offensive cyber warfare capabilities. While unable to contest US military power globally, China has substantially increased the risks to America of maintaining a military presence in the Western Pacific.

The US faces a dilemma: while wanting to be a faithful ally, it doesn't want to hand its security partners a blank cheque in contesting China's claims

Third, Beijing began probing the limits of US credibility as an ally in the Pacific. By applying carefully calibrated pressure around territorial disputes in the South China Sea and the East China Sea, China was testing how closely the US would back up allies such as the Philippines and Japan over uninhabited islands and reefs. Here the US faces a dilemma: while wanting to be a faithful ally, it doesn't want to hand its security partners a blank cheque in contesting China's claims. Between 2012 and 2016 a game of brinkmanship and signalling occurred in the Western Pacific as intense and consequential as any during the Cold War. By the time Beijing eased off the pressure, the score was one-all: the United States had been seen to support Japan but not the Philippines to face down the Chinese challenge. Beijing must be well pleased: the disquiet among American allies such as South Korea and Australia, and unspoken concerns about the limits of American commitment, have spread far beyond the countries directly involved in confrontations with China.

Reimagining Australia in the new world order

To Asian policymakers, it's obvious that the pattern of international power is shifting. It's understandable and probably inevitable; as in the past, the region will reorient itself. Just as these policymakers read American power in material, not moral, terms, so they understand China's surging power in matter-of-fact ways. It's a laconic view of power that only a long-term, cyclical conception of supremacy and decline can impart.

Australia needs to be similarly dispassionate about the way power is shifting in its region. The advent of Trump calls for a fundamental rethinking of Australia's strategy towards the Asia-Pacific. Such a rethink has long been needed, but with Obama and his predecessors, we hid behind a hope that American power and resolve would prevail once again. Trump tears away any excuse for wishful thinking. For the past quarter-century, Canberra's policy has been to support American primacy and US efforts to prevent the rise of rivals. Trump's election forces us to confront the failure of that policy and the implausibility of the restoration of America's position of dominance. Rather, Australian policymakers must acknowledge the overwhelming reality that our future will increasingly be shaped by Beijing, not by Washington.

The Australian debate on the US alliance misses the point entirely. We should neither summarily break the alliance nor blindly deepen our investment in it. We should keep the alliance with the US but reshape it towards ensuring an enduring American role in the emerging Asian power balance, just as we reshaped the alliance towards a different rationale at the end of the Cold War. We need to become as unromantic about American power as our northern neighbours. American power will endure, but the US will no longer be the arbiter of the regional

Reimagining our foreign policy is going to be the hardest thing we've ever done

order. We should therefore make sure that we use our alliance with the United States to help secure what we regard as an acceptable and achievable environment in the Asia-Pacific. But first that requires working out what we want.

Reimagining our foreign policy is going to be the hardest thing we've ever done – because this is the first time since European settlement that Australia has had to contemplate living in a region not dominated by a culturally similar ally. For all of its talk of "shared destiny," nothing about contemporary China gives cause for confidence that a Beijing-centred regional order will be sympathetic to our values or interests. Nor can we have much confidence that other regional powers will combine to enforce the principles of stability, access and equality that have been so important to our safety and prosperity.

The first challenge is to let go of the belief that only American primacy can ensure an acceptable regional order. The government's mantra of upholding the rules-based order is an exhortation to regional countries to rally around the flagging superpower and help buttress the status quo against China. But the longer we profess faith in American primacy, the harder it is to prepare for the new era already begun. We've drawn a rhetorical line in the South China Sea to which few regional countries have been willing to commit. Even Canberra has been reluctant to step up to join the US Navy in its freedom of navigation exercises, which require sailing within 12 nautical miles of Chinese artificial structures.

Next, we need to get used to thinking about power as countries in the Asian region do. For most of them, American power was not inherently a good thing. It was useful because it provided stability and predictability without being too onerous. American power made fewer demands in Asia than in Europe or Latin America; it was mostly unconcerned about the nature of domestic regimes, human rights or economic governance, nor was it inclined to make sudden geopolitical démarches. This means the countries in the region that have developed security partnerships with Washington – including India, Indonesia and Vietnam – have not done so from an admiration for US values or a desire to bolster US primacy in the region. They have built relationships with the US because they believe America can help them develop their own capabilities, giving them the credibility and confidence to resist Beijing's growing assertiveness.

In most of the region's capitals, there is resigned acceptance that China will become the dominant power in Asia, alongside a hope that China's dominance will not be any more onerous than America's. But at this stage it remains a hope. There is substantial disquiet in the region about the arbitrary way China uses its power and its condescending dismissiveness towards those with differing interests. Nor has the United States or any other country found a way to deter or shape China's assertive behaviour. And few really believe that Beijing's "core interests" will stop at the South China Sea.

So the key question confronting Australian policymakers is the same that confronts their counterparts in Asia: how can China's power be moderated in ways that allow space and voice for other regional countries? At the moment there is little coordinated thinking about this. The region confronts a geopolitical version of the fable of the blind men and the elephant: each man describes the elephant based on the part of the animal he can feel. Each country is so preoccupied with its own challenge in managing China that it has little inclination for thinking in collective terms about this question.

Even Japan, the Asian neighbour most alarmed about China's power and intentions, and the most energetic in working to preserve the status quo, has given up on the thought of moderating China's behaviour. Tokyo is in balancing mode – encouraging other countries to build the capacity and summon the will to push back if China's demands continue to expand. For now, Prime Minister Shinzō Abe's efforts are focused on outreach to India, Australia and South-East Asia, and the revival of the concept of a quadrilateral security dialogue between the US, Japan, India and Australia.

This is unlikely to work. The traditions of non-alignment run too deep; the complexities of bilateral relations with Beijing are too consuming; the capabilities and interests of regional countries are too diverse. Our best hope is not for some grand coalition to balance China, but for each of China's larger neighbours to assert its interests when they are challenged. China is wealthy and powerful, but it is in a crowded neighbourhood; not one of its frontiers – from India in the west to Japan in the east – is geopolitically uncomplicated. In recent years, Japan, Vietnam, Indonesia and India have each stood up to China, confidently but not provocatively. At a time of transition, these assertions of resolve are important – they are noticed not only in Beijing but also in other regional capitals. The best hope of moderating China's behaviour is to convince the country that every time it acts arbitrarily or coercively, it increases its neighbours' willingness to push back.

This is where we need the United States to play a vital role in bringing about a new equilibrium in the Asia-Pacific. America will have a role not only in Asia's balance of military power but also in continuing to shape the principles of regional order. It is very much in our interests that Washington, supported by countries such as Australia, Japan, South Korea and Singapore, uses its influence to champion ideas such as freedom of navigation, an equal voice for all countries, and the importance of clearly articulated and generally supported rules. American places and bases in the region, including its training facilities in Darwin, will continue to play an important role in anchoring a stabilising American presence in the region.

Australia's alliance with the US undoubtedly gives us both the capabilities and the confidence to push back against those of Beijing's activities we object to. This will become harder as China's power grows relative to America's; that is why we have started exploring our capabilities and techniques of asserting

We need the United States to play a vital role in bringing about a new equilibrium in the Asia-Pacific

our interests. Last year's shifts of policy and tone, from blunt public statements about Chinese interference to the strong language in the Foreign Policy White Paper about the South China Sea and the call for Beijing to respect smaller countries, showed Canberra testing the limits of how far it can assert its independent interests.

But we should be deploying the alliance in other ways as well. We should be talking to the United States about its vital role in fostering an emerging power balance in the Asia-Pacific. At the same time, we should be discussing with our regional neighbours where their – and our – non-negotiable interests lie, and how best to assert these when challenged. We need to be talking with our neighbours about what a China-dominated region will mean for their and our interests, and where the points of resistance and influence with China may lie. This is going to be difficult and politically sensitive, particularly since countries such as Indonesia, India and Vietnam are deeply committed to traditions of non-alignment. And we should be urging China intensively to think about its power in terms not of pre-eminence but of finding a stable equilibrium in a complicated neighbourhood. This is going to be tough. It will mean finding the right format that allows both sides to escape the largely sterile and formulaic script they have used thus far. The relationship will need to be more intimate, which will allow the communication to be more direct.

Talking to the United States about shifting to a balancing role in Asia would have been a difficult conversation to have in Washington before Trump's inauguration. Americans see their power and their alliances in moral terms; any doubts about US primacy or instrumental approaches to alliances in the past have been met with accusations of disloyalty. Trump is different. His rhetoric on China may have been tough, but his actions have been accommodating. He wants more independent allies, and for him every relationship is renegotiable. Finding a new American role in Asia, where the US works alongside its allies but doesn't take responsibility for ensuring regional order, is a deal the Donald just might make. ■

NORTH KOREA'S MISSILE STAND-OFF

The risk is real:
Prepare for war

Kim Beazley and L. Gordon Flake

The coldest winter

In the northern hemisphere this has already been one of the coldest winters for a very long time – a piece of good fortune for the Winter Olympics in South Korea, even though it may be the last happy moment on the Korean Peninsula for a long time. A war there is a distinct possibility, and some form of military action to disrupt North Korean nuclear weapon developments is even more likely. Diplomacy may have run its course. Without doubt we are at the most dangerous moment since the armistice that adjourned the Korean War in 1953. A war today could have unimaginable consequences: a catastrophic death toll, missile strikes beyond the Peninsula, the first nuclear bombs to be used in conflict since Hiroshima and Nagasaki. The risk has long been real – and in 2018, with Donald Trump in the White

House, it is alarmingly high. Events unfolding on the Peninsula and in Washington are pointing in a direction that is difficult, but essential, to contemplate.

Until now, the most dangerous moment since the 1953 armistice occurred in 1994, when the current North Korean dictator's father, Kim Jong-il, foreshadowed the development of a nuclear reactor capable of producing fissile material and evicted international inspectors. In the ensuing crisis, the US Secretary of Defense, William J. Perry, gave President Bill Clinton options for a "surgical strike" on the reactor site. This provoked the US ambassador to South Korea, Jim Laney, and the commander of US Forces Korea (USFK), General Gary Luck, to suggest to Clinton that American non-combatants in South Korea would first need to be withdrawn. This, they warned, might well cause Kim to pre-empt a strike with military actions of his own. Their sobering conclusion was that this would result in tens of thousands of civilian casualties. A large proportion of the civilian population in and around the South Korean capital, Seoul, lived within 80 kilometres of the border with North Korea. Now the figure is over 50 per cent. Effectively, these South Koreans were hostages to North Korean good behaviour. They still are.

That fear of mass civilian casualties and the perception that North Korea has a low bar on pre-emption have haunted US administrations. At least ten major North Korean atrocities and provocations since 1967 have been essentially passed over. Most recent was the sinking of the warship ROKS *Cheonan* in 2010, which killed forty-six South Korean sailors, and the artillery shelling of Yeonpyeong Island later that same year. More importantly, North Korea has proceeded with the construction of nuclear weapons (perhaps including hydrogen bombs) and the further development of short-range, medium-range and, most recently, intercontinental ballistic missiles as potential delivery systems. The response has been sporadic attempts at diplomacy, backed by ever-tightening sanctions on products capable of supporting the North Korean program. The sanctions have intensified, with more direct impact on the economy as a whole. The Obama administration, motivated by a fear of mass casualties, as well as a paucity of good options and a hope that at some point the North Koreans would bend, articulated the Allied tactic as "strategic patience." The Trump administration has said those days are over.

The enemies

What has changed since 1994? The first shift has been the emergence of Kim Jong-un after his father died in 2011. Kim Jong-un is clearly the most insecure of the dynastic line. His regime is marked by regular and brutal purges of his retinue and deepening oppression of his people. He has articulated this unsurpassed brutality in his attitude not only towards South Korean governments but also to his neighbourhood. For example, in September 2014 a North Korean committee stated, "The four islands of the [Japanese] archipelago should be sunken into the sea by the nuclear bomb of Juche. Japan is no longer needed to exist near us." Kim has made clear that the development of his intercontinental ballistic missile (ICBM) capability is aimed at rendering the United States politically impotent on the Peninsula, confident that Washington would not sacrifice American cities to defend its southern ally.

Unlike those of his predecessors, Kim Jong-un's nuclear capabilities are entwined with his legitimacy. Recognition of North Korea's status as a nuclear power is non-negotiable. Last year saw twenty-three tests of missile capability, culminating in the launch of the Hwasong-15 ICBM. At that point Kim declared his program "complete," preceded as it was by his sixth nuclear test in September of a possible thermonuclear device.

Kim's New Year statement for 2018 attracted attention for its outreach to South Korea after two years of no communication, an obvious attempt to drive a wedge between the United States and its ally. The outreach produced a flurry of diplomacy to incorporate the North in the winter games. For some, this raised hopes. But for most observers, there was the sense that the Peninsula had been in that place before and none should be fooled. More significant was his indication that this year North Korea will focus on "mass producing nuclear warheads and ballistic missiles for operational deployment."

Likely preying on Kim's mind is the fact that his conventional forces as well as his people have made sacrifices to achieve his objective. Indeed, last year he indicated he needed to do something about that. His grandfather's conventional military superiority vis-a-vis the south has massively eroded. The size of his army (more than twice South Korea's) is not matched by its capability. Much equipment is obsolete, and there are reports of breakdowns and shortages of spares, while South Korea's equipment is up-to-date and constantly renewed. When in 2010 North Korea fired 170 shells at Yeonpyeong Island, 25 per cent failed to explode. The situation would be worse now. In a conventional battle, Kim would be at a massive disadvantage. His biological and chemical capabilities – if not his nuclear capabilities – would have to be used early, but on a fast-moving battlefield these unconventional weapons are unlikely to be militarily effective. All this amplifies the significance of whatever nuclear capabilities he has. It heightens his sensitivity to any threat to those capabilities. And it deepens his tolerance for even the toughest sanctions.

Unlike those of his predecessors, Kim Jong-un's nuclear capabilities are entwined with his legitimacy

The second major change in the Korean situation is the election of US president Donald Trump. His approach to national security has deviated more from his 2016 election campaign promises than any other set of his policies. In many ways, his "America First" campaign – and his isolationist rhetoric – was conducted in a way that made him the "peace" candidate. He dismissed allies, including South Korea, even suggesting at one point that they might feel free to provide their own nuclear umbrella. He sensed his voter base was tired of American commitments and wars, yet now finds himself on the verge of a war that would dwarf any in recent times.

Trump is not motivated by empathy for the South Korean people but by the threat of a North Korean ICBM capable of hitting US cities. In response to Kim Jong-un's 2017 New Year's speech, which laid out the DPRK's intention to develop an ICBM capability, then President-elect Trump responded with a signature tweet: "It won't happen!" And his reactions since have been dominated by that belief. Writing in December 2017, the *Sunday Times'* Washington bureau chief, Toby Harnden, quoted a State Department source saying resignedly that Trump "has shown no grasp of the complexities and inherent dangers of military action on the Korean peninsula."

Trump's grasp of most matters in international politics and military affairs is rudimentary. His interventions, by tweet or otherwise, provoke instant mockery among the informed community. But he is the man in charge and so they bear close analysis. They reveal his method of processing the information and intelligence he is receiving. His reaction to the Hwasong-15 test – "It is a situation we will handle. We will take care of it" – was mocked for its characteristic bravado, yet can also be seen as full of menace, particularly as viewed from Pyongyang. In his 2018 New Year's address, Kim said: "It's not a mere threat but a reality that I have a nuclear button on the desk in my office. All of the mainland United States is within the range of our nuclear strike." Trump's tweet in response was: "Will someone from his depleted and food starved regime please inform him that I too have a Nuclear Button, but it is a much bigger & more powerful one than his, and my Button works."

Again, most commentary mocked this schoolyard exchange. As a track to Trump's thinking the most significant part of his tweet was "and my Button works." This was a telling claim. Trump is the first American president to seriously contemplate a war to disarm North Korea of its weapons. What this reflects is a sense Trump has that North Korea is not where it claims to be, even if it could get there. In other words, he perceives a window of opportunity, but one his advisers tell him is closing. The Chinese are taking him very seriously. They are constructing camps to house the millions of refugees they might expect from a war and moving troops to the border. Those troops are not there to intervene decisively in a war; they don't have those capabilities. They are there to assist with the refugees. Chinese president Xi Jinping, in his first visit with Trump, lent weight to the view that North Korean capabilities were not as advertised. Following a year of extensive North Korean testing, opposed by the Chinese, they clearly see the game is moving rapidly and have joined serious sanctions against Pyongyang. Knowing Kim's devotion to his weapons, they have been trying to shift the agenda to something less than total North Korean disarmament. They know they can't control him, but are desperate to produce a workable American negotiating position.

> **Trump is the first American president to seriously contemplate a war to disarm North Korea of its weapons**

The man in the middle

It would also be folly to assume that President Trump's threats of "fire and fury" are limited to him and not widely held in the administration. US National Security Advisor H.R. McMaster, who has termed North Korea "the greatest immediate threat to the United States" and repeatedly focused on the fast-closing window for a strike, is a leading proponent of action. This has posed some unique challenges for US Secretary of Defense Jim Mattis, who understands the scale of a likely conflagration. He has repeatedly warned that a conflict with North Korea would be "catastrophic," while at the same time providing assurances of the ultimate outcome – total US victory and the end of Pyongyang's nuclear program – so as to maintain deterrence.

As Secretary Mattis is working out, argument about North Korean weaknesses is a double-edged sword. On the one hand it is essential to buy time for diplomacy. Yet, processed through Trump's worldview and the state of his knowledge, it suggests military opportunity. Still, it has to be made, and Mattis does his best. After the Hwasong-15 launch he said that the missile "has not yet shown to be a capable threat against us right now."

Retired lieutenant-general Patrick O'Reilly, a physicist, former director of the US Missile Defense Agency and senior fellow at the Atlantic Council, expressed similar scepticism about the Hwasong-15. He observed that the North Koreans keep shooting the missile almost straight up, and not in the parabolic arc of a standard missile trajectory, which is harder to achieve. "There are some really ill-informed technical suppositions that have been made," O'Reilly told CNN about assessments that the 28 November missile could menace the US mainland. "When I hear in one or two years they could have an operational capability that could hit Washington ... people are making very, very aggressive assumptions. There's a lot left to be done before you can assess a credible threat."

Mattis emphasises his work in tandem with US Secretary of State Rex Tillerson to achieve a diplomatic solution through a tighter sanctions regime. Mattis matters to Trump. Tillerson doesn't. Likewise, South Korea barely counts. Trump was furious when President Moon Jae-in suggested last year that he had a "veto" over a pre-emptive US attack. Likewise, he was furious over a Tillerson suggestion that the United States was prepared to talk to North Korea about talks without preconditions. Trump is more on song with his UN ambassador, Nikki Haley, who stated in January this year: "We consider this to be a very reckless regime. We don't think we need a band-aid and we don't think we need to smile and take a picture. We think we need to have them stop nuclear weapons and they need to stop it now."

For years the Pentagon has worked on military options to pre-empt North Korea. These are probably the most up-to-date of contingency plans the US has. Further, they have been regularly exercised with the South Korean armed forces. They are based on a detailed understanding of the disposition of North Korean forces. Most analysts are sceptical that the US knows where everything nuclear is: something would be held deeply disguised and thrown in last-minute desperation as the regime faced destruction. US surveil-lance capabilities are exponentially greater than the public, and most commentators, appreciate. Nevertheless, the risks of massive dev-astation, at least on the Peninsula and in Japan, are real. Trump's principal source of advice now is the Pentagon. Its primary duty is to work out how things can be done, a different task from saying whether they should be. Those, like State Department officials, who carry the diplomatic argument are sidelined. That leaves Mattis in the weighty position of having to find both a solution and the enabling argument.

The battle options

While speaking to the Aspen Security Forum in July last year, General Joseph Dunford, chairman of the Joint Chiefs of Staff, made a little-noted but very revealing contribution on Pentagon thinking. Faced with the prospect of a million-plus dead and the ruination of South Korea, Japan and probably the global economy, he adopted a sub-tle change of tone, away from a scenario that ends in unsustainable, unimaginable damage:

> I would shift that slightly and say it [pre-emptive war] would be horrific ... But it is not unimaginable to have real options to respond to North Korean nuclear capability. What's unimag-inable to me is allowing a capability that allow a nuclear weapon to land in Denver, Colorado ... So my job will be to develop mili-tary options to make sure that doesn't happen.

Well, how would that be done? Here, Mattis, an advocate of diplomacy, has to undermine the diplomatic position. Not in the public mind, but perhaps in Trump's. Mattis has said the United States has some potential options that would not see the devastation of Seoul. The details, understandably, he would not provide. Journalist Toby Harnden reported a discussion in the Pentagon last year attended by specialists and business leaders that suggested the use of joint CIA and special forces teams, much like the Operational Detachment Alpha 574 that was used in Afghanistan to seize the nuclear sites.

This is not easy to foresee. One would expect an infinitely better performance from the North Koreans than from the Taliban. A covert operation would probably

The risks of massive devastation, at least on the [Korean] Peninsula and in Japan, are real

not be a standalone activity. Extensive use of bombers and cruise missiles is likely to play a part. Crucial here would be the trigger – perhaps a response to a North Korean reaction to an actual naval blockade, which North Korea has said would be an act of war. More likely, a reaction to a foreshadowed nuclear or ICBM test. North Korea has suggested it will conduct an atmospheric hydrogen bomb test in the Pacific. That would guarantee a US response. Or, more probable, an effort to perfect the ICBM. North Korea is nowhere near a viable capability without further testing. The possibility of a broader war through an accident or misinterpretation of posturing around these events is substantial.

What would be the North Korean reaction to a limited punitive event? If Kim is as "rational" as is commonly claimed for him, a cruise missile strike to pre-empt a test would hardly see a massive response. Most likely, a hit at a soft South Korean target or military base, or a cyberattack. The problem is this: neither this limited initiative nor a wholesale assault on North Korea's nuclear capabilities could be attempted without having in place the mechanisms for an all-out war. Limiting the damage on Seoul would require the rapid degrading of the mortar, rocket, missile and artillery capabilities ranged against it. Given the degrading of North Korean conventional capabilities, that might be doable. The problem would lie in what Kim would do in a situation where his regime's survival, which he identifies with his nuclear weapons, was in question. Has he secreted nuclear weapons that could unleash devastation in the south and Japan? Half a dozen weapons would be economy-destroying; a dozen would be civilisation-destroying. South Korea has enough shelters (7000) to house the population of greater Seoul. However, there have been limited preparations. Exercises are derisory and the population has had no sense of urgency about personal preparation. Trying to divine Kim's responses and the evolution of this battle is like trying to define "a very complex game of three-dimensional chess in terms of tic-tac-toe," according to veteran strategist Anthony Cordesman of the Center for Strategic and International Studies.

That brings us back to the question of why Trump would try. For him, the game is simple. North Korea shall not have an ICBM. For the experts and advisers advocating a pre-emptive strike, it gets back to what sort of nuclear power North Korea is. North Korea is a nuclear power like no other, and its intentions are an open question. Does North Korea desire a nuclear capability simply for deterrence and regime survival, or does it have a more aggressive ambition to use that capability to try to reunify the Peninsula? None of the other nuclear powers has seen its weapons as defining its government's legitimacy. Nor do they see them as a cover for aggressive foreign policy intent (though this may be changing with Russia). In Kim's case, his regime survival is threatened not only by American capabilities but also by South Korea's existence as an alternative social model. Back in the early days of his grand-

North Korea is a nuclear power like no other, and its intentions are an open question

father, North Korea was the economic power on the Peninsula. Now it is dwarfed by the south. With the United States out of the equation, coercion of South Korea may be a viable option.

The fallout

It is difficult to imagine that a pre-emptive US strike (perhaps excepting a very limited one) can do anything other than risk the devastation of South Korea and perhaps Japan with dreadful human consequences – ones that are ruinous to South Korea and Japan, and very consequential for China. And then there are the massive environmental consequences. Small wonder former Trump strategist Steve Bannon, before leaving the White House, said, "There's no military solution, forget it."

Australia is on the sidelines but is likely to be affected and possibly engaged. We have interests here beyond our alliance with the United States. We have strongly supported the non-proliferation regime globally and have seen its success as crucial to security and stability in our region. South Korea, Japan and China are critical trading partners, and in different ways we care deeply for their people. Ruin for them is ruin for us. Independently of the alliance at the time of the 1953 armistice, we signed a guarantee to aid South Korea in the event of an unprovoked attack from the north. Pre-emption would be a fast-moving game. South Korean and US forces are well placed and planned without us, but we may be approached. The US has come to value us for niche first-class capabilities. One comes to mind: our Wedgetail battle-management aircraft, now in Iraq and Syria, are superior to anything the United States has and could be rapidly deployed. It is hard for us to insert ourselves into the diplomacy here. We have supported maximum pressure on the Kim regime. Apart from looking for opportunities to inject ourselves, we will remain largely sidelined, but with much invested in the outcome.

There is a closing, not closed, window for diplomacy. Any attack would need to be preceded by a comprehensive diplomatic strategy for China. China would need assurances and offers – perhaps a withdrawal of any US forces post-conflict to the south of the current border between North and South Korea. Trump – and certainly his advisers – might want to test the waters with China and North Korea on solutions involving a major stand-down rather than entire elimination of North Korea's nuclear capability. We probably have not yet seen the full weight China is capable of bringing to bear on North Korea. It would have to be a great deal to bring Kim to heel, and it is difficult to envisage such an outcome that would not undermine his sense of his regime's legitimacy.

It is not yet midnight, but as the crisis deepens, the diplomatic and military options get more and more complex. In averting catastrophe, having a bigger nuclear button will not guarantee success. That is obvious to most informed observers. But is it obvious to Trump? That is unknowable. What is certain is that his sense of legitimacy is bound up in North Korea credibly having no ICBMs. The chairman of the Council on Foreign Relations in New York, Richard Haass, a very experienced analyst and member of the Bush administration, puts the prospect of war at fifty-fifty. The prediction is chilling. This is going to be a hard year. ■

> **It is not yet midnight, but as the crisis deepens, the diplomatic and military options get more and more complex**

CAN AUSTRALIA FIGHT ALONE?

The cost of the military's US dependency

Andrew Davies

Over the next decade, Australia is preparing to invest almost A$200 billion in defence capability. This includes plans for new warships, submarines and fighter jets, as well as long-range rockets, drones and various armoured vehicles for the army. The outlay is substantial, and will add to the country's military edge and see it among the world's top fifteen defence spenders. But there is one thing this outlay will not achieve: a self-reliant military.

Despite an increasingly uncertain strategic environment, with challenges ranging from the North Korean missile crisis to tensions over Taiwan and the South China Sea, Australia's growing military spending won't give us an ability to defend ourselves independently. We will continue to rely on larger and more powerful friends to supply us with military technology and help out with logistics, and, in the case of a conflict with a major power, to come to our direct assistance. In addition, though it's not often explicitly discussed, we will continue to shelter under the US nuclear umbrella.

There are different ways to think about defence self-reliance. The hardline definition would be an Australian defence force that sources all its equipment and maintenance support from Australian-owned firms. Nobody thinks that's a realistic prospect for Australia: we have a small population from which to generate the resources required for defence self-reliance, but we have a continent to defend, as well as the 10 per cent of the world's oceans that fall under our jurisdiction. Our workers enjoy relatively high wages, which tends to make labour-intensive projects expensive, and the government takes a relatively low tax cut by OECD standards, which limits its spending ability. Worldwide trends also suggest that, increasingly, only the very largest economies can aspire to go it alone in the development and manufacture of top-end military equipment. The number of global arms firms is dwindling, and it is much harder for new entrants in smaller countries to compete.

Instead, Australian military planners aspire to a more limited goal: having adequate combat forces to defend Australia, but remaining dependent on external suppliers for hardware and logistical support.

In making the case for spending on the local defence industry, the government sometimes argues that this will not only help to achieve greater self-reliance but will also be a sound investment in the national economy. The numbers suggest otherwise, and such spending is only worthwhile if it can be justified on strategic grounds – that is, if it makes Australia less vulnerable and more secure.

A reliance on foreign suppliers is a vulnerability that could mean the difference between winning and losing a war. But it also comes with advantages: it allows Australia to buy cutting-edge weaponry from established production lines in larger countries that can better afford to produce them. And it effectively allows us to pool our research and development risks with partners that have larger defence industries.

The question, then, is how self-reliant Australia's military needs to be. That is the quandary facing Australia as it decides whether to pay more for self-reliance – and therefore whether to spend less on, say, health, welfare or education.

Ultimately the answer depends on the costs of varying degrees of self-reliance, on where Australia thinks it will fights its next war, and on who the enemy is likely to be.

The ADF: Made in the USA (and elsewhere)

Having a military that depends on other countries to provide critical elements of its capability necessarily constrains our freedom of action and narrows the options available to the Australian government in a crisis. If self-reliance were cheap and easy to develop, we'd take as much of it as we could get. But it's neither cheap nor easy, so we either have to accept that we depend on foreign suppliers and governments for defence equipment and know-how, or we need to be prepared to spend a lot of money to get there.

When it comes to arming itself, Australia is starting from a low base. The Australian Defence Force (ADF) sources its most important fighting platforms from overseas – mainly the United States and the European Union. The army's tanks and artillery have "Made in the USA" stamped on them. Every aircraft type operated by the Royal Australian Air Force (RAAF) comes from overseas, as do the weapons, sensors and communication links needed to employ them in combat operations. And that isn't just the case for acquisition. We also rely heavily on foreign firms and contractors for maintenance and logistics. Australia's top twelve defence firms (by contract value) include the local arms of multinationals BAE (UK); Raytheon, Boeing and Lockheed Martin (US); Thales (France); and Airbus (EU). The only local supplier and supporter of warfighting equipment in the top twelve is the Adelaide-based ASC, which is building warships and maintaining the Collins-class submarines. And the Collins, despite being built and maintained here, also relies on American and European suppliers for support of its sensors, combat system computers and weapons.

The list goes on. We import virtually all the data links, computers and communications systems that process and move around the data that the ADF, like all modern militaries, depends on for its effectiveness. In the early 2030s we'll start replacing Swedish-designed submarines with French-designed ones – and both rely on American combat systems and weapons for their effectiveness. Whichever of the three contenders for the navy's future frigate is chosen, it will be a foreign design, with many of the key systems being sourced from elsewhere (though not all – the radar will be an excellent Australian product, and a component of the combat system will also be indigenous; see Table 1).

Table 1: Australia's major military systems

	YEAR IN SERVICE	COST 2016	PLACE OF BUILD	FOREIGN-SOURCED SYSTEMS
Collins submarines	1996	$10 billion	Australia	Weapons (US) Combat system (US) Sensors (France, US) Propulsion (Europe)
Air warfare destroyers	2017	$10 billion	Australia	Weapons (US) Combat system (US) Sensors (US, UK) Helicopter (US) Propulsion (US)
Future submarines	2032	> $50 billion	Australia	Weapons (US) Combat system (US) Sensors (TBD) Propulsion (TBD)
Future frigates	2027	> $30 billion	Australia	Weapons (US) Aegis combat system (US) Propulsion (TBD)
Super Hornet strike fighter	2010	$6.9 billion	US	All
F-35 joint strike fighter	2021	$15 billion	US	All
Air-to-air refuelling aircraft	2011	$2.4 billion	Europe	All
Artillery	2010	$400 million	US	All
Bushmaster vehicles	2005	$1.25 billion	Australia	Battle management system (Israel) Weapons (US) Communications (France) Propulsion (US)

It's important to distinguish between having some local industry capacity and achieving genuine independence: even when we build warships and military land vehicles here, most of the equipment that makes them effective warfighting platforms is sourced from somewhere else. Despite some truly world-class Australian defence products, as well as examples of local improvements to imported systems, there is no credible path to a homegrown ADF.

The line between victory and defeat

A nation's warfighting capability ultimately depends more on the total resources that it can bring to bear than on the extent of its homegrown defence capacity. But any reliance on external suppliers carries a risk, and history contains some good examples of third parties being able to influence the way in which combatants use their military capabilities. In some cases, such as the Falklands War, it has probably made the difference between winning and losing.

In April 1982 the UK government decided to retake the Falkland Islands from Argentina by force. At a special Saturday sitting of the House of Commons, British prime minister Margaret Thatcher declared: "British sovereign territory has been invaded by a foreign power ... It is the Government's objective to see that the islands are freed from occupation and are returned to British administration at the earliest possible moment."

The United Kingdom was a staunch Cold War ally of the United States and, along with Australia, Canada and New Zealand, is part of the global Five Eyes intelligence collection network. Argentina, on the other hand, wasn't a US ally, but had the support of many of the members of the Organization of American States, a regional grouping spanning North and South America. The United States faced the prospect of a serious downturn of its diplomatic relationships with the Spanish-speaking states in its own hemisphere. As a result, the first official American position on the conflict was that it wouldn't take sides.

No American forces took part in the Falklands War. But, as events unfolded, the United States effectively ended up taking a side by providing critical support to the British in supplying missiles and anti-submarine warfare equipment, resupplying fuel to the British airfield at Ascension Island and providing intelligence support. Although it was a war against a relatively modest adversary, it's likely that Britain couldn't have won without American help.

It was a different story on the other side. The Argentine forces might well have won the war if they had received support from the United States or France. The Argentine Air Force was equipped with a mix of aircraft from different sources, but the ones that did the most damage to British ships were American-supplied Skyhawks and French Super Étendards. Neither of them were able to perform at the highest level of capability. The Skyhawks were in pretty poor shape after six years of an American embargo on spare parts. The Étendards, though in much better condition, were limited by a shortage of ammunition. They were the only Argentine aircraft able to launch Exocet missiles – another French export product – but only five of the air-launched version of the missile had been delivered when the conflict began.

The French, conflicted by a war between a NATO ally and a good customer, decided that strategy trumped business. Further sales of weapons were embargoed, and the French and British worked together to prevent Argentina from procuring any more Exocets through third parties. That was just as well – the small number of Exocets that were available managed to sink a crucial transport ship and a British destroyer, as well as damaging another. If Argentina had been able to source more Exocets, it could have threatened the entire British operation, which was already a close-run thing.

The experience of both sides in the Falklands War shows how vulnerable a military can be to interruptions of supply if it's dependent on a third party for vital equipment. But that's the situation for most countries today – only the biggest powers are entirely self-sufficient in military equipment. Australia is not an exceptional case in that respect, and it's worth understanding how we got to this situation. Our indigenous aviation industry makes a good case study.

The rise of the global arms giants

Australia has had its own experience of being at war and discovering that its strategic priorities were not shared by the countries supplying it with equipment. Because they opposed the US-led intervention in Vietnam, both Sweden and Switzerland refused to supply equipment to Australia during the Vietnam War. When the Australian

Army's stocks of ammunition for the Carl Gustaf anti-tank weapon ran low, the Swedish government publicly refused requests to supply more (though there are later reports of back-channel deliveries being arranged). And Switzerland withheld the delivery of the last of the Pilatus PC-6 Porter light aircraft to the army, despite the delivery having been contracted. Neither of those embargoes threatened national survival, or even the outcome of the conflict – Australia was hardly going to alter the outcome of the Vietnam War with some extra cases of ammunition and another light aircraft (though our troops probably faced elevated risks).

Only the biggest powers are entirely self-sufficient in military equipment. Australia is not an exceptional case

A much more serious case occurred in 1942. After the fall of Singapore and the Japanese occupation of Papua New Guinea and Indonesia, the Australian government had reason to worry about national survival. The air defence of northern Australia became a high priority after many Japanese bombing raids staged out of occupied territories to our north, and there were fears of Pearl Harbor–type attacks by carrier-borne aircraft against major centres further south. But Australia's allies had their own problems, and urgent requests for the supply of frontline aircraft from Britain (our traditional source of aircraft at the time) and from the United States were only partially successful. Our own aircraft design and construction capability was ramped up dramatically, and got as far as producing a couple of indigenous designs that saw service during the war, though both depended on American engines.

By the end of the war, Australia's designers were up there with the best, and the capacity of our local industry had been built up substantially by manufacturing thousands of foreign-designed aircraft here under licence. As it happened, we would have got through without a local design capability, because both the tide of war and the availability of aircraft from Britain and the US changed in our favour before the local designs came online, leaving them as a footnote in the story of the air war.

Despite the vulnerability experienced in 1942, and the shock to the national psyche of coming under direct attack, the ready availability of advanced designs from overseas suppliers saw local advanced design capability steadily wound back in the decades that followed. In the 1950s Australia managed to put a British engine into the American-designed Sabre, which required some substantial redesign work, to produce a unique Australian variant. But by the 1980s our ambitions had diminished to the local assembly of American-produced F/A-18 Hornets. A generation later, we find ourselves buying the more advanced Super Hornet "off the shelf" from US production lines, and making components for the F-35 Joint Strike Fighter that will equip the RAAF out to 2050.

That's not an unusual story, and it's mirrored across comparable countries. Canada persevered with its own combat aircraft designs into the 1960s, and still has a government-supported civilian aircraft design and construction industry. But ultimately the costs of developing new military jet designs proved too high. Those costs have to be written off over the production run, and Canada simply didn't need enough aircraft to make it worthwhile. Meagre export sales couldn't make up the difference. The larger numbers being fielded by the US military gave American firms across the border a huge competitive advantage. Canada, like Australia, yielded to the inevitability of economic forces and became a consumer of the much larger industrial capability of the US.

New Zealand has gone one step further. While there has long been a local civil aviation industry, the Royal New Zealand Air Force has always operated aircraft sourced offshore. But the rising cost of frontline military aircraft made the replacement of its 1960s vintage Skyhawks in the early 2000s unviable (or, more accurately, unable to attract sufficient priority in the limited defence budget), and the decision was made to retire the fast-jet capability altogether.

Australia yielded to the inevitability of economic forces and became a consumer of the much larger industrial capability of the US

Of the English-speaking allies outside the US, only the UK has persevered with a substantial capability to develop its own aircraft. But even there, in a little over half a century Britain has gone from being number three in the world (after the US and the Soviet Union) to being a partner in multinational consortia or a purchaser of foreign designs (the UK is another customer of the Joint Strike Fighter program). Britain's partners in pan-European designs include industrial powerhouse Germany, which has also shied away from the eye-watering costs of developing its own aircraft.

That reflects a continuing trend of the consolidation of a once diverse global industry into a small number of key players. The US remains by far the most active producer and exporter of arms, with the European Union and Russia also having substantial market shares. Coming off a low base, China and South Korea are also starting to make inroads into the global market.

Even with significant export success, the industrial landscapes within the US, the EU and Russia have been characterised by a sharp reduction in the number of arms firms, mostly through acquisition by larger firms and mergers. For example, only nineteen of the top 100 US aerospace and defence companies in 1991 still exist today. In Western Europe a handful of big players dominate the market. Two of the biggest are the UK's BAE Systems and the Paris-based European Aeronautic Defence and Space Company. To compete with US giants Lockheed Martin and Boeing, the two European firms attempted to merge in 2012, but were blocked by their governmental owners. It is always going to be difficult for countries such as Australia to compete in an ecosystem dominated by giants: Lockheed Martin's 2015 revenue was US$46 billion, compared to spending of US$2.4 billion across Australia's entire defence sector.

The growth of the giant multinationals has led to a reduction in choice for buyers of military equipment. Lockheed and Boeing have produced more than 6000 F-15 and F-16 strike fighters and have exported them widely, including F-16s to many European customers. The multinational (UK, Germany, Italy and Spain) Eurofighter has had some export success, but the total production to date is under 600. A couple of Western European countries have opted to go it alone and produce an indigenous frontline strike fighter, in the form of Sweden's Gripen and France's Rafale – the product of the only such standalone programs in the past thirty years. (And even then the Swedish product employs a derivative of an American engine.) They are both good performers, and both

It is always going to be difficult for countries such as Australia to compete in an ecosystem dominated by giants

have found some international buyers. But, so far, the combined production run has been just 407, affording lower economies of scale than for the American aircraft.

Nonetheless, Sweden's and France's homegrown products are sometimes brought up in defence circles to argue for government support for a much more sophisticated local defence industry. Both countries manage to produce their own submarines, warships and combat aircraft, and both are successful exporters of defence equipment. Why, then, so the argument goes, can't Australia do the same?

The glib answer is that we can, if we want to badly enough. A better answer is that we can, but we're unlikely to want to badly enough to pay the costs required to do so. To understand why, we need to take a look at the wider economic picture.

Wasting money on Australia's defence industry

It's tempting to conclude that building up the local defence industry will necessarily spawn all sorts of wider economic benefits – and you don't have to look far to find that argument being made. Here's Prime Minister Malcolm Turnbull on the subject in 2016:

> There is no question that this is a matter of profound national importance, that as far as possible we use our defence dollars to drive Australian industry, Australian innovation, because the benefits go well beyond the defence budget.

But that might be confusing cause with effect. Extra in-country defence spending isn't likely to deliver much in the way of – to quote Malcolm Turnbull's favoured mantra – "jobs and growth." It's unlikely that local spending will propel Australia's defence industry to the cutting edge of best practice, or compensate for the loss of many thousands of manufacturing jobs in areas such as car production. In fact, the most likely outcome is that an inefficient industry will detract from the overall economy – it would be a minor miracle if we ended up with a high degree of defence self-reliance.

It's true that many northern European countries have advanced industrial sectors that contribute to their prosperity. That's due to several factors: they had the historical accident of being early to the Industrial Revolution, they have well-educated populations, and they have 600 million prosperous consumers not far away, with few trade barriers. That gives them a huge comparative advantage in advanced manufacturing. Taking that view, we start to see why Australia made the decisions it did after World War II – we had a very small local market for expensive manufactured goods, but huge world markets for food and the raw materials to rebuild after a long and ruinous war. In other words, we did the rational thing and developed the economic sectors that deepened our comparative advantages. It's no coincidence that our agricultural and resources sectors are among the most sophisticated in the world.

In contrast, our manufacturing sector is relatively small, and our defence industry is a small component of that. Table 2 on page 58 shows the relative size of our industry, manufacturing and defence industry sectors. A glance at the figures will show that the defence industry has its work cut out if it is to give the sort of national boost the prime minister and the minister for defence industry, Christopher Pyne, have been talking up. Even a defence industry twice the size of today's would represent only 1 per cent of the national industrial sector. And rapid growth in the defence sector would almost inevitably pull skilled people from elsewhere, including the broader manufacturing sector. As the numbers in Table 2 show, the defence industry is relatively poor at generating revenue and adding value. So a government-driven push to grow the defence sector is likely to reduce the net output of the economy.

Table 2: The relative size of the Australian defence industry in 2015

	AUSTRALIAN INDUSTRY	AUSTRALIAN MANUFACTURING SECTOR	AUSTRALIAN DEFENCE INDUSTRY
Employees	10,636,000	856,000	25,000
Revenue ($billion)	3113	383	6.7
Value add ($billion)	1066	98	1.7
Revenue per employee	$292,669	$447,487	$268,000

Source: *ABS figures via ASPI analysis in Mark Thomson,* The Cost of Defence 2017–18.

Getting in first also confers an advantage. The Europeans (and other nations) already selling high-end military equipment into the world market aren't going to stop doing so if Australia manages to bootstrap its own defence industry. Australian exports would have to displace other suppliers in developed markets. If we can't generate substantial exports, then we'll be wearing all of the research, development and management overhead costs ourselves, spread over the small number of units our own forces need. So the government is betting – despite implausibly long odds – that growing the defence sector will improve its efficiency relative to the rest of the Australian industry, and then push big international exporters, such as BAE, Airbus, Boeing and Lockheed Martin, out of their well-established markets in Europe, the Middle East and Asia.

That said, it's possible that Australian defence exports will grow. Some Australian defence technologies have made an impact on the world market. We've been selling missile decoys for warships to the United States and Canada for a couple of decades, and we've exported Bushmaster Protected Mobility Vehicles to the United Kingdom, the Netherlands and several other smaller customers. The radar being fitted onto our existing and future frigates is an outstanding performer, and it wouldn't be surprising to see it sell well. But these are isolated instances, and won't generate the revenue necessary to justify the government's plan to pursue economic growth by boosting the defence industry. More importantly, none of the examples goes anywhere near making Australia self-reliant for our defence materiel.

But even strong export growth would be coming off a low base. According to the Stockholm International Peace Research Institute, Australia currently ranks nineteenth on the list of defence exporters by value (and ninth as an importer). That tends to exaggerate the scale of the local enterprise. The top ten arms-exporting countries account for 90 per cent of the total activity in the sector. Australia's share of the global arms market is less than half of 1 per cent.

Aggressively pursuing arms sales also has associated political and moral hazards. Trying to sell to other Western countries or to advanced Asian nations such as Japan and South Korea is the hardest way for Australia to climb the ladder of suppliers. All of those prospective customers have their own defence sectors they are anxious to protect (and quite a few also think they are going to export their way to great defence self-reliance). There are other markets, particularly in the Middle East, but some arms sales are more ethically and geopolitically fraught than others. So far the government hasn't encountered too much resistance to its "growth through defence" ambitions, but Australian-supplied weapons turning up on the "wrong" side of a conflict on the evening news might change that.

Australia's vulnerabilities in future conflicts

The fact that we're unlikely to get the promised economic benefits from government investment in the local defence industry doesn't necessarily mean that such investment is a bad idea. If there's a strategic payoff from being able to do more for ourselves, it could still make the investment worthwhile. As we saw in the Falklands War example, being on the wrong side of a supplier's politics can lose a war. The two key questions are whether Australia is likely to find itself in a war that hinges on our ability to produce defence equipment locally, and whether we can insure against that by investing more in local industry. If the answer to that second question is "yes," the smart thing to do would be to invest in self-reliance.

To decide whether buying military equipment at a premium – which is what developing and building it ourselves usually comes down to – is worthwhile, we need to think about the wars that Australia could credibly find itself in over the years to come. That sounds a bleak way to fill in an afternoon, but it's routine for defence planners, and for governments when they sign off on future equipment purchases.

There's plenty of hand-wringing about the current strategic situation in Asia, and much of it for good reason: a war on the Korean Peninsula looks depressingly possible; China's annexation of territory in the South China Sea has increased regional tensions; Taiwan remains a potential flashpoint; and competing claims to islands in the East China Sea by Japan and China remain unresolved. In the event of a conflict, could Australia's vulnerability to its foreign supply chains leave us short of military capability?

American involvement in Australia's possible future wars is an important factor because so much of our front-end air and maritime capability is of US origin. In many ways we have built a defence force around the assumption that American engagement in our extended region is a given – as evidenced by the many assertions of continued US regional pre-eminence to be found in the 2016 Defence White Paper.

Could Australia's vulnerability to its foreign supply chains leave us short of military capability?

Less than two years after the publication of that paper, there is a live debate about how reasonable assumptions about continued American engagement in the Asia-Pacific are. For now at least those working assumptions appear to be holding. After the first year of Trump's "America first" doctrine the US remains an active Asia-Pacific power, and most of the potential flashpoints in our extended region continue to engage US interests. So US engagement is likely to continue in the short to medium term but, as defence analyst Hugh White frequently points out, the longer-term trends are against it.

But even a more isolationist America that has largely decamped from Asia would be unlikely to actively oppose Australia's military engagements in the region to the point of cutting off support to Australia's forces. With one plausible exception to be discussed later, Australia would have to misplay its hand badly to get so offside with Washington as to imperil resupply.

A more likely vulnerability is relying on equipment sourced from players far from the Asia-Pacific. For example, given China's economic clout and Europe's fragile economic growth, it's possible to imagine Beijing leaning on European suppliers to withhold support for Australia's defence forces. A dependence on European equipment, such as the Air Force's Airbus air-to-air refuellers, could see our military capability compromised. That's one reason for Australia to look to the United States for equipment: we both have strong interests in the Asia-Pacific and we tend to agree on the features of the international order that we value.

If Australia were to find itself in a conflict without the direct combat support of the United States but with an assured resupply of arms, self-reliance would take on a different character – it would mean being able to field forces that do not have to rely on the US or other coalition partners for in-theatre logistical support. Some of the NATO countries participating in the air campaign over Libya in 2011 demonstrated that combat capability relies not just on having the right equipment on day one but also on having enough depth for a sustained campaign. Despite the limited nature of that conflict, British and French aircraft relied heavily on American refuelling capability and intelligence support, and ran out of precision-guided weapons within a month. Similarly, and despite being ready to take on substantial combat roles, Australian forces in Afghanistan often had to rely on US or NATO helicopters for movement and fire support because none of our armed reconnaissance or utility helicopters were fit to be deployed.

Conversely, Australia's forces sent to contribute to recent air strikes over Iraq and Syria have self-deployed, have decent stocks of weapons, and have taken their own air-to-air refuelling and airborne radar aircraft with them. Instead of being an operational burden on the United States, Australia's contingent has sometimes been able to step in and support other coalition forces.

> So what sort of war could we envisage ourselves trying to prosecute with no support from the United States?

None of those things come cheaply: Australia has spent many billions of dollars on developing the capability to go to war with largely self-sufficient forces. It would cost even more to free our forces from relying on foreign suppliers. So what sort of war could we envisage ourselves trying to prosecute with no support from the United States or the other suppliers of ADF equipment? There's no sensible scenario that has us taking on a substantial power a long way from home. Despite

Australia's oft-stated interest in maintaining the "rules-based global order" – an assertion liberally sprinkled through both the defence and foreign White Papers – there's simply nowhere outside our immediate region where our interests are more substantial than those of other nations. As has been the case historically, in a war outside our neighbourhood, Australian expeditionary forces wouldn't be alone.

That leaves only our near neighbourhood (the arc of nations from Indonesia around to the South Pacific) – the one part of the world in which our interests generally run deeper than those of other players. There are precedents for thinking we could have to go it alone there: in the past couple of decades, Australia has either resolved or been called on to use its military forces in peacekeeping and stabilisation operations in Timor Leste, Bougainville and the Solomon Islands. Looking further back, Australian forces came to blows in Malaya in the 1950s and with Indonesian forces in the 1960s (and could have again if Indonesia had taken a different stance during the 1999 Timor operation). Regional peacekeeping operations typically require only light land forces. While the 6000-strong deployment to East Timor strained the ADF's resources, there was little call on the international supply lines for top-end equipment.

Which takes us to the only credible scenario in which we might need greater self-reliance: extensive operations in our near neighbourhood. Of nearby countries, only Indonesia has extensive military forces, so the discussion effectively boils down to that one possibility: war with our northern neighbour. And it's certainly conceivable that

Never again miss an issue. Subscribe and save.

☐ **1 year auto-renewing print and digital subscription** (3 issues) $49.99 incl. GST (save 29%).

☐ **1 year print and digital subscription** (3 issues) $59.99 incl. GST (save 15%).

☐ **2 year print and digital subscription** (6 issues) $114.99 incl. GST (save 20%).

☐ Tick here to commence subscription with the current issue.

ALL PRICES INCLUDE POSTAGE AND HANDLING.

PAYMENT DETAILS I enclose a cheque/money order made out to Schwartz Publishing Pty Ltd. Or please debit my credit card (MasterCard, Visa or Amex accepted).

CARD NO. ☐☐☐☐ ☐☐☐☐ ☐☐☐☐ ☐☐☐☐

EXPIRY DATE _____ / _____ CCV _____ AMOUNT $ _____

CARDHOLDER'S NAME _____

SIGNATURE _____

NAME _____

ADDRESS _____

_____

EMAIL _____ PHONE _____

Freecall: 1800 077 514 or +61 3 9486 0288 email: subscribe@australianforeignaffairs.com **australianforeignaffairs.com**
Digital-only subscriptions are available from our website: australianforeignaffairs.com/subscribe

An inspired gift. Subscribe a friend.

☐ **1 year print and digital subscription** (3 issues) $59.99 incl. GST (save 15%).

☐ **2 year print and digital subscription** (6 issues) $114.99 incl. GST (save 20%).

☐ Tick here to commence subscription with the current issue.

ALL PRICES INCLUDE POSTAGE AND HANDLING.

PAYMENT DETAILS I enclose a cheque/money order made out to Schwartz Publishing Pty Ltd. Or please debit my credit card (MasterCard, Visa or Amex accepted).

CARD NO. ☐☐☐☐ ☐☐☐☐ ☐☐☐☐ ☐☐☐☐

EXPIRY DATE _____ / _____ CCV _____ AMOUNT $ _____

CARDHOLDER'S NAME _____ SIGNATURE _____

NAME _____

ADDRESS _____

EMAIL _____ PHONE _____

RECIPIENT'S NAME _____

RECIPIENT'S ADDRESS _____

RECIPIENT'S EMAIL _____ PHONE _____

Freecall: 1800 077 514 or +61 3 9486 0288 email: subscribe@australianforeignaffairs.com **australianforeignaffairs.com**
Digital-only subscriptions are available from our website: australianforeignaffairs.com/gift

Delivery Address:
LEVEL 1, 221 DRUMMOND ST
CARLTON VIC 3053

Australian Foreign Affairs
REPLY PAID 90094
CARLTON VIC 3053

Delivery Address:
LEVEL 1, 221 DRUMMOND ST
CARLTON VIC 3053

Australian Foreign Affairs
REPLY PAID 90094
CARLTON VIC 3053

the United States and others mightn't want to take a side if we manage to get into such a conflict. Much would depend on what was at stake, as was the case when the United States and others didn't place a high value on whose flag flew over the Falkland Islands, and wanted to keep both sides in the positive column of the diplomatic ledger. If Australia and Indonesia came to blows over something less than existential issues, we could find ourselves lacking broader support (and might deserve to be cut off for not being able to manage our diplomatic affairs better).

And if major powers wanted to stop us, they have tools other than interrupting the supply of arms. When Britain, France and Israel took military action against Egypt in the Suez Crisis of 1956, the United States was seriously unimpressed, and made clear that it was prepared to use economic leverage against its erstwhile allies. Britain was especially vulnerable to US threats to sell off the federal treasury's holdings of pound-sterling bonds. Given Australia's reliance on foreign funds and revenues from trade, that sort of threat would get the attention of any Australian government.

Resisting the push for extra defence spending

Because of the near impossibility of being able to independently provide our armed forces with a full suite of indigenously designed and produced equipment, Australia will likely always be vulnerable to the interruption of supply of defence materiel. The good news is that there is no obvious reason to worry much about the reliability of those arrangements.

Nonetheless, there is growing momentum for a greater defence spend overall, and for more of the defence budget to be directed to local industry. That position is partly motivated by a deteriorating strategic situation, and partly by parochial industrial and political interests. But much of that thinking is predicated on shaky assumptions. Even with a substantial boost, the local defence industry isn't big enough or broad enough either to provide an economy-wide boost, or to give us the ability to be independent of foreign suppliers for much of our military equipment. Increasing the defence budget with those goals in mind could see us spending a lot – with pain to be felt elsewhere in the government's budget – for relatively little gain.

The good news is that we don't need to do it. The Australian economy should continue to do well without relying on the defence sector. And our armed forces can do everything they are likely to be asked to do, whether in coalition operations far from home – in which case, we're likely to be alongside our major suppliers – or operating alone in our own backyard, which tends to be less demanding, at least in terms of sophisticated capabilities. We should do all we can to try to maintain this situation because if we ever need to develop a capability to fight a major conflict alone, the challenges will be immense and the costs considerable. ■

LETTER FROM WASHINGTON

The Trump effect

David Kilcullen

Two days after Donald Trump was elected, I was having dinner in a Middle Eastern country with an American diplomat – a tough senior Obama political appointee, with hard-fought policy achievements to her name – when she burst into tears mid-conversation. Like the entire commentariat, and virtually everyone in the US political establishment (including, arguably, Hillary Clinton), she had so taken for granted Clinton's impending elevation that the election hit her like a physical blow. Now she was watching her role in a Clinton administration evaporate; she'd been crying on and off, she said, for days.

She wasn't the only one. Celebrities (scores of whom promised to move to Canada if Mr Trump won, but later discovered they'd been joking), feminists who regarded Trump's victory as an assault from a revenant patriarchy and activists who mounted last-ditch legal challenges to deny him the presidency were inconsolable. Bernie Sanders' supporters were torn between outrage and schadenfreude, claiming their boy could have won if he hadn't been robbed in the primary. Women marched in nationwide protests alleged to outnumber the inauguration crowd (the real crowd, not President Trump's imaginary one, which numbered millions, in what his adviser Kellyanne Conway dubbed "alternative fact"). The Resistance – a loose movement viewing Trump as dictator-in-waiting, including factions willing to oppose him "by any means necessary" – was born.

A year after the election, Resistance members, their ranks thinned by the passage of time and Trump's failure to enact any major part of his agenda, gathered to howl at the moon. I mean this literally: all over the country, people gathered, turned their faces to the evening sky and howled. The president's manifest ignorance of governing seemed to have found its perfect mirror in an incoherent opposition. Hillary Clinton's book tour for *What Happened*, her sorry-not-sorry campaign memoir, drew sellout crowds. Punters coughed up US$600 a head for choreographed events free of any key self-revelation. I've never heard of an author charging for a book talk, but this was clearly not really about selling books: these were less literary than expiatory rituals, their grief-stricken attendees simply a more cerebral version of the moon-howlers.

Moral panic, impotent rage and existential despair – call it the "Trump effect," the 2017 equivalent of 2009's "Obama derangement syndrome" – was in full flight. Along with the belief that President Trump is a uniquely dangerous fascist, adherents of this view consider his administration a wholly owned subsidiary of the Kremlin, and believe his incompetence (and of course the Resistance) is all that stands between America and the abyss.

A Republican tribal variant – the "Nevertrumpers" – sees the administration as illegitimate, viewing the president (with some justification) as a lifelong Democrat who mounted a hostile takeover of their party, is trashing its principles and is manifestly unfit for office. During the campaign, dozens of Republican defence and foreign-affairs experts, representing their party's core policy cadre, signed letters disavowing Trump. A few later renounced this thoughtcrime and came crawling back, or expressed astonishment that the White House subsequently turned elsewhere for talent, but most are sitting out the administration in a principled, if somewhat pouting, manner.

I want to offer a different take on the Trump presidency, from the rather oddball perspective of an expat Aussie with no partisan affiliation within US politics, who has lived in America for a decade, and has served as a career official (i.e. not a political appointee) in the Bush State Department and as a consultant to the Obama administration (and who, full disclosure, is very happily married to an Obama political appointee, former Undersecretary of the Navy Dr Janine Davidson). I come neither to bury Trump nor to praise him, but to suggest that his administration, rather than uniquely incompetent or illegitimate, might be an upside-down duck. Let me explain.

I don't own this metaphor: it belongs to Dr Colin Kahl, one of the smartest foreign-policy professionals in the Obama administration (or, to my knowledge, any other), who was the national security adviser to Vice President Joe Biden and headed the Pentagon's Middle East portfolio. His image is the best I've heard to explain what's going on. Where President Obama's administration was once described as the proverbial duck – serene on the surface, paddling like hell underneath – Colin's view is that the best anyone can hope for is that Trump's might become an upside-down duck, with sound and fury above the surface, in the president's tweets and public appearances, but with professionals quietly executing the business of government below the waterline. In this interpretation, the president's public breaches of decorum would mask a conventional policy program. The administration would be a fairly normal Republican one, just with a stylistically unusual chief executive. I'm not sure I completely buy this interpretation (and neither does Colin), but it's a useful tool for getting beyond appearances in an administration whose surface has been especially distracting. So let's run with it for a bit, and see where it takes us.

As Janine has written, most US presidents come into office focusing on domestic issues, with merely a casual interest in foreign policy and defence. As she points out, that's perfectly understandable, since presidents get elected by a constituency that primarily cares about domestic matters. Still, most new presidents rapidly realise they have little control over domestic policy, and turn their attention overseas by the end of their first term. President Trump is entirely typical of this pattern, though he seems to be following it at a rather accelerated clip. His signature policies (withdrawing from the

Trans-Pacific Partnership, renegotiating the North American Free Trade Agreement, banning travel from terrorism-affected countries, exiting the Paris climate agreement) all focused externally from the outset – though, characteristically, they were tailored to generate support from interest groups in his base. The failed initiatives of his first year – Obamacare repeal, infrastructure upgrades, creating coal and manufacturing jobs, alleviating the opioid crisis – have, again typically, been largely domestic.

In foreign policy, his actual policy decisions (as distinct from his personal demeanour) have been fairly conventional. His decertification of Iran's compliance with the 2015 nuclear deal, for example, got a lot of criticism, but meant nothing in the international context (certification is an internal US requirement

Trump's presidency might become an upside-down duck, with sound and fury above the surface ... but with professionals quietly executing the business of government below the waterline

that was imposed on President Obama by Congress against his will, and has no effect on the agreement). Even while decertifying Iran, President Trump didn't actually withdraw from the deal, no doubt having been advised by his policy team that, as just one of six signatories, pulling out would leave the deal intact but render Washington unable to influence it. Decertification did, however, score points with his base – which, as with most of his other moves, seems to have been the whole point. Again, though, this is largely a matter of style: most if not all presidents find domestic considerations driving their foreign policy. Mr Trump is simply less subtle about it than most.

Likewise, his decision to recognise Jerusalem as Israel's capital and begin moving the US embassy there from Tel Aviv is less of a departure than it seems (or than the hyperventilation from Democratic or Nevertrump commentators suggests). Trump's announcement – which amounted to little more than acknowledging the law of the land in the United States since the mid-1990s, and the reality on the ground since the 1960s – was less radical than it appeared and was motivated by a desire to deliver on a promise for a key campaign constituency (evangelical Christians). The difference here is not policy content, but the fact that Trump – charmingly naive as this might seem – is actually following through on a campaign promise.

The policy continuity between the Trump and Obama administrations is notable, but not particularly unusual. All administrations find themselves confronting circumstances they didn't fully understand on the campaign trail, once read into the classified intelligence sources only available to incumbent governments. Most candidates drop their more inconvenient or impracticable policies once the election is over. Mr Trump has done some of that (the proposed 45 per cent tariff on Chinese imports is an example), but his attempt to keep some commitments, such as the Mexican border wall, suggests he's unusually attentive to following through on promises, most likely because his extraordinarily low popularity and failure to persuade independents and Democrats means he can ill afford to alienate his base.

Likewise, his strategy on Afghanistan, panned as aggressive war-mongering, was actually quite mainstream in policy terms, though that policy was buried under militaristic bluster. As I watched his speech, I wondered how Biden must feel about Trump stealing his policy from 2009, which was criticised at the time – by Democrats – as too weak. Trump's plan was almost identical to Biden's: light-footprint counterterrorism, reliance on drones, the use of air strikes and special forces to suppress terrorists and stop them from attacking the United States, willingness to negotiate with the Taliban, pressure on Pakistan, moving from a withdrawal timeline towards a sustainable footing. The only difference was President Trump's rhetoric. His plan was basically Biden's with harsher language – a difference of style, not substance.

Ditto for the "defeat" of Islamic State in Syria and Iraq. Candidate Trump's bluster about targeting terrorists' families, carpet-bombing cities and refusing to rule out tactical nuclear weapons drew condemnation. But in office he persisted with Obama-era policies, continuing campaigns against Mosul and Raqqa that Obama started in 2015, interfering little in the decisions of military commanders appointed by his predecessor, and taking credit for developments that were long-planned or outside anyone's control. His most criticised action – ramping up air strikes, which brought a spike in civilian casualties – echoed President Obama's massive expansion of the drone campaign, and arguably shortened the conventional phase of the conflict, perhaps even indirectly saving lives.

Speaking of which, far from being defeated, Islamic State is alive and well, with key cadres intact and an expanded footprint outside Syria and Iraq. It has simply (and temporarily) dropped back into guerrilla mode after the failure of its conventional war of manoeuvre, so President Trump now faces the identical problem President Obama confronted before the 2014 ISIS blitzkrieg. Again, other than harsher language and a somewhat shakier grasp of the facts, there's little to distinguish this president's approach from his predecessor's.

On North Korea, again, President Trump is continuing a long-standing US approach – lean on Beijing to control Pyongyang; apply sanctions to discourage the nuclear program; bolster South Korea and Japan with exercises, missile defences and garrisons; and ramp up US missile defences – that goes back (with minor variations) to presidents Obama, Bush and Clinton. This has been failing for twenty-five years, and is as unlikely to succeed in "denuclearising" the Peninsula, especially since North Korea is now a nuclear state with intercontinental ballistic missiles, and there's no imaginable set of circumstances under which Kim Jong-un's hereditary dictatorship would give them up. To be sure, President Trump's insulting rhetoric ("Little Rocket Man," "short and fat," "fire and fury") is something from which previous presidents have shied away. But considering the baroque insults North Korea traditionally hurls at Western leaders, and Trump's legendarily thin skin, it seems to have had little effect.

If anything, his insults may have had a positive impact, if reports of North Korean diplomats wandering the halls of the United Nations in New York, looking to open a back-channel to the administration, are to be believed.

On that note, here's a radical thought: what if not everything that comes out of the president's mouth is idiotic by definition? Trump promises a border wall and ridiculously claims he'll force Mexico to pay for it, and undocumented immigrants crossing the southern border drop to the lowest level since 1971. He boorishly cranks up the rhetoric on North Korea, and the United Nations and China impose unprecedented sanctions on Pyongyang. He heartlessly bans travel from countries with inadequate screening for terror suspects – using an identical list to that proposed in 2015 under Obama – and several make major improvements to their vetting systems. He refuses to endorse Article 5 of the North Atlantic Treaty until members meet their own funding commitments – outrageous! – and several laggard countries start increasing defence budgets towards the 2 per cent GDP target, something the last two presidents repeatedly asked for but failed to achieve. What if the difference in style not only masks unexpected policy continuity but is actually effective in its own right?

> **Here's a radical thought: what if not everything that comes out of the president's mouth is idiotic by definition?**

That's as may be, but – moving beyond the duck metaphor for a moment – the president has also clearly departed from political norms in ways that have hurt his agenda and the country's reputation. From Australia's standpoint, these could have significant negative consequences in our own region and beyond.

In effect, the new administration shows a high degree of policy *continuity* with its predecessors, but a disturbing lack of *consistency* across its various branches. In our region, this lack of consistency is most apparent – and damaging – in the area of China policy. The Obama administration's "pivot" (actually, it was called the "rebalance") to Asia was panned as a purely rhetorical reorientation after a decade of tunnel vision on terrorism in the Middle East, but at least it provided a policy framework for different departments – the Pentagon, the intelligence community, the State Department and aid agencies – to work coherently. In contrast, on issues such as China's expansive presence in the South China Sea, North Korean nukes, Taiwan, trade policy and regional defence engagement, not only are there multiple competing power centres in the current administration but the president's position has proven remarkably changeable and contradictory. This has led different agencies to pursue independent, even competing, agendas. It has created confusion and forced allies to further question the future of the American regional security guarantee that has underpinned growth and stability in the region.

In violating norms of politics, most egregious is President Trump's shaming and bullying of cabinet members, including Jeff Sessions as attorney general and Rex Tillerson at the State Department. Tillerson is alleged to have described the president as a "fucking moron," one of the few signs of pushback from a secretary of state who has repeatedly clashed with Trump on policy issues and been left humiliated by presidential tweets. No foreign minister can influence other countries unless their leaders believe he has the president's confidence and speaks with his authority; Tillerson clearly does not. UN ambassador Nikki Haley in New York seems to be running her own foreign policy independent of Tillerson's – without any intervention from Trump – leaving partners uncertain where exactly policymaking authority lies. For allies such as Australia, that increases the risk of supporting US positions – a fact that clearly underpins the focus on self-reliance in Australia's recent Foreign Policy White Paper, "Advancing Australia's Interests." Trump's neutering of Tillerson has also contributed to a collapse of morale at the State Department. Combined with the failure to even nominate candidates for hundreds of political appointments in the executive-branch departments, this means that, whatever your view of the president's agenda, his ability to execute it is increasingly questionable.

Likewise, Trump's public trashing of Jeff Sessions – one of his earliest supporters – not only undermines Sessions' reputation, but also makes it harder for the attorney general to advance the president's agenda with America's fifty states and 17,000 law-enforcement agencies. President Trump, it seems fair to say, lacks an intuitive grasp of the fact that loyalty goes both ways. Again, this message – and the mercurial disposition it signals – raises costs and risks for allies. The mooted nomination of Admiral Harry Harris, the pro-Australian commander of US Pacific Command, as the next ambassador to Canberra is seen by some in Washington as a means of reassuring Australia of American support. But if the president casually slams his own cabinet members and undermines his own secretary of state, what substantive difference does the president's choice of ambassador make?

Another norm President Trump has ignored is his violation of the spirit (though not the letter) of an anti-nepotism law enacted after President John F. Kennedy's appointment of his brother Robert as attorney general. By appointing relatives (including his daughter Ivanka and her husband, Jared Kushner) as key policy advisers, the president encourages foreign diplomats in the capital to ask a question normally only relevant in third-world autocracies: should we work with appointed officials of the government, or go around them to deal directly with the family? Certain ambassadors – it would be tactless to name them – have become adept at cultivating the Kushners, for example, further disempowering the cabinet and the executive branch, and creating the parallel, informal power structures normally associated with banana republics. Australia can play this game as well as anyone, and better than most – but as a long-standing treaty ally with enduring institutional, economic and cultural ties going back more than a century, we shouldn't have to.

Politicising the judiciary and law enforcement – starting with the president's tweet claiming a judge would be unable to render a fair verdict due to his Mexican heritage; continuing with the pardon of Sheriff Joe Arpaio, a famous immigration hardliner; and peaking with his denigration of the FBI and Department of Justice – has been another damaging Trump departure. To be fair, Trump had some solid precedent: President Obama's use of the IRS to target opponents in the 2012 campaign, Attorney General Loretta Lynch's tarmac meeting with President Bill Clinton at the height of an investigation into his wife's illicit email server, and FBI director James Comey's multiple interferences in the 2016 presidential race are cases in point, along with a string of recent revelations of politicisation within the FBI and the justice department. Again, President Trump seems to be departing from his predecessors' behaviour not so much in substance, but in lack of subtlety.

President Trump seems to be departing from his predecessors' behaviour not so much in substance, but in lack of subtlety

One area where the president *has* departed from recent practice is his selection of numerous military men for cabinet or senior non-cabinet posts. Marine generals James Mattis for Defense and John F. Kelly for Homeland Security, army generals Michael Flynn and H.R. McMaster as successive national security advisors, and General Kelly's move to White House chief of staff have raised concern about civil control of the military, or militarisation of policy. With the notable exception of Flynn, this concern is tempered by the idea that military officers are the "grown-ups in the room," an "axis of adults" (to quote Kahl again) restraining the president's impulses – a role described to me by a friend as "continually trying to stop a toddler from playing in traffic"; Senator Bob Corker, one of the president's most vocal Republican opponents, called it "adult day care."

In my view, this makes the prevalence of military officers in the upper reaches of government worse, not better. Far from reinforcing civil control, it puts the highest elected civilian official in the country under the de facto regency of an unelected military elite. Political scientists looking at this set of circumstances in a foreign country would call it a praetorian or "securitocratic" state, which – despite best intentions – is clearly not where the world's greatest democracy ought to be heading. Again, this is not to critique the officers involved, all of whom I know, and all of whom, I believe, are as conflicted about this as anyone else.

From Australia's point of view, the officers in key roles are all friends – John Kelly and Jim Mattis, in particular, are very familiar with Australia's circumstances, positively inclined towards our shared interests, and determined to maintain an effective presence in the region and beyond. But, at some level, that doesn't make it better – for America's longest-standing regional ally, institutional and structural connections ought to matter more than the personalities of individuals hired and fired on the whim of a mercurial, startlingly ill-informed president. This comes home most clearly in the issue of nuclear strategy.

President Trump, as commander in chief, is never more than a dozen steps away from the "football," a briefcase containing a communications system and launch options for a nuclear strike. In the nuclear arena, as in almost no other, the president has virtually unlimited authority, with few checks and balances – especially in the case of response to an incoming nuclear attack, when he might have as few as four minutes to order a launch. Given the president's escalating tit-for-tat rhetoric with Kim Jong-un, and Kim's continued missile launches that now seem able to place a nuclear weapon anywhere in the United States (and therefore anywhere in Australia), concern over this recently prompted Congress to review the president's nuclear launch authorities. From my (admittedly parochial) viewpoint, this suggests a useful rule of thumb: if we feel uncomfortable about President Trump exercising a particular power, perhaps we should ask whether any president ought to have it.

There's a silver lining to all this, believe it or not. Most presidents bring three kinds of people into office – operatives from their political parties, members of their personal entourages, and their party's "bench" of policy experts, who normally occupy positions in think tanks or academia while the other party is in power. Hillary Clinton would have been typical in this respect, drawing in thousands of campaign staffers and appointees (such as my tearful diplomat friend) as well as the Democratic Party establishment and a deep policy bench. In the interest of continuity, she also would likely have kept on large numbers of Obama appointees.

Trump, of course, had no campaign structure to speak of, and his policy staff verged on the non-existent, so he had no personal entourage to bring in – other than, of course, his family, which explains their prominence. Likewise, being spurned by the Republican establishment, he had no policy bench to fall back on. And the Republican National Committee bureaucrats he brought in – prominently, Reince Priebus and Sean Spicer – quickly fell victim to conflicts within Trump's inner circle, driven by political bomb-thrower Steve Bannon, himself ousted after a few months.

The result is that a slew of Democrat policy experts and political operatives, disappointed in their expectations of a job under Hillary, left government. But where they would normally have filled Washington think tank slots vacated by Republicans coming into the administration, they couldn't – those slots are still occupied, by Nevertrumpers and conservative Republicans whose hatred of Trump rivals the Resistors'. As a result, many of the finest younger leaders in the Democratic Party have moved out of Washington to other cities, breaking the bubble between the capital and the country. Others – more than twenty, at last count – are running in the 2018 midterms or in state and local elections across the country, bringing a much-needed infusion of new blood to their party. Whatever your political orientation, in a system that relies for its stability on two strong competing political parties, this can only be a good thing – especially since, if the 2016 primary battles teach Democrats anything, it should be that their party is in dire need of younger talent and a closer connection to America's heartland.

One reason many Republican national security experts declined to serve in the administration, beyond personal distaste, was the ongoing stink of collusion with Russia that has hung around the new president and his former campaign staffers. It's worth pointing out that, more than a year after President Trump's election, congressional and special counsel investigators are yet to release any evidence of direct collusion. At the same time, US intelligence had already concluded in January that there was a Russian intelligence operation aimed at undermining Hillary Clinton, eroding confidence in the electoral outcome and creating a window of disruption to enable Russia to improve its position in Ukraine, Syria and elsewhere under cover of post-election paralysis. The Russian

Ironically, the main loser from the Russian influence operation is likely to be Vladimir Putin

spooks who organised that operation are almost certainly astounded by how long the disruption has lasted, fuelled by a reflexively anti-Trump media, President Trump's self-defeatingly thin skin, and the Democrats' need for a scapegoat after their stunning election defeat. Ironically, the main loser from the Russian influence operation is likely to be Vladimir Putin, who now faces harsher policies on Ukraine, stronger sanctions on his cronies and greater restrictions on his financial interests than he did under President Obama's de facto appeasement policy.

None of this is to excuse President Trump's louche, swaggering ignorance, or the Berlusconi-like debasement of American politics that accompanied his election. This debasement is at least as much his opponents' fault as his own, but barring a catastrophic nuclear exchange (there's a phrase I never thought I'd have to write) there will be other presidents. This too shall pass, as President Lincoln said. For Australia and other allies, the uncertainties of alliance politics are greater than usual, but then so is the motivation to become more self-reliant, capable and independent in our defence and foreign policy – and that too is a good thing, both for Australia and ultimately for the United States. And anyway, as I've argued here, not everything about the Trump administration is bad, or even particularly unusual – it may simply be that the duck, for once, is upside down. ■

Reviews

Asia's Reckoning: The Struggle for Global Dominance
Richard McGregor
Penguin Books

After enjoying a royal welcome in Beijing late last year – complete with a tour of the Forbidden City at sunset and a full military parade in Tiananmen Square – Donald Trump declared that he and Xi Jinping had "great chemistry."

The Chinese president, for his part, was less magnanimous. Xi told his American counterpart that the Pacific was big enough for the both of them – a dismissive line that reflects his belief that he heads a rising power while Trump leads one in decline.

Flattery versus disdain. The remarks neatly encapsulated the seismic shift taking place in Asia.

The United States, the supreme power in the Pacific for some seven decades, is now run by an impulsive president who has shown little appreciation for America's old alliances. China, meanwhile, is led by an increasingly authoritarian leader who sees his country as a global power with a glorious, millennia-long history that is returning to its rightful place in the world. Neighbouring North Korea is ruled by a ruthless dictator who's made astonishing advances towards having a deliverable nuclear arsenal. And in the middle is Japan, an American ally and a Chinese rival, a nation that modernised while China disintegrated but is now in denial about the countries' reversal of fortunes. Even amid a demographic crisis it has no idea how to fix, Japan still sees itself as an economic colossus and is unwilling to concede its decline.

In his excellent new book, *Asia's Reckoning*, Australian journalist Richard McGregor writes that the competition between these two Asian powers, exacerbated by Trump's unpredictability, should alarm the rest of us. "Any clash between China and Japan would not be a simple spat between neighbours," writes McGregor. "A single shot fired in anger could trigger a global economic tsunami, engulfing political capitals, trade routes, manufacturing centers, and retail outlets on every continent." That, of course, includes Australia, a country torn between its long-standing alliance with the United States and the commercial opportunities of a rising China.

McGregor is uniquely placed to draw together these themes. He spent two decades in Asia, reporting from Tokyo, Shanghai and Beijing, and was the *Financial Times'* bureau chief in Washington, D.C. (he was the bureau chief in

Beijing while I was the paper's correspondent in Seoul, and we worked together in Washington). Drawing on his experience, McGregor has written a magisterial book that combines old-fashioned shoe-leather reporting – he conducts interviews with major players in Japan, China and the United States – and extensive archival research to chart seven decades of relations between the three countries. These relations, he shows, are more complex than suggested by the prevailing view of China versus the US–Japan alliance. He recounts the line by China's first premier, Zhou Enlai, that China and Japan had enjoyed "two thousand years of friendship and fifty years of misfortune," and recalls Henry Kissinger's disdain for his Japanese counterparts, as well as Japan's constant fear that the United States will desert it. "The Japanese have always been paranoid that the United States and China are natural partners – big, boisterous continental economies and military superpowers that wouldn't hesitate to bypass Tokyo in a flash, if only they could find a way to do so," he writes.

At the book's centre is the growing rivalry between China and Japan – and the risk of a confrontation that an overstretched America will struggle to deal with. Even before Trump came to office and disrupted the old way of doing things, Xi and Japanese prime minister Shinzō Abe, both fierce nationalists, were locked in a battle for influence and supremacy. They took office only a month apart, at the end of 2012, just after Japan had nationalised a group of rocky islands known as the Senkaku in Japan and the Diaoyu in China. Xi was radically different from his notoriously dreary predecessor, Hu Jintao, and had an ambitious plan to make China great again. One of the first things Xi did was to whip up antipathy towards Japan, recalling late nineteenth- and early twentieth-century events such as the Nanjing massacre.

In 2015, ahead of the seventieth anniversary of the "Chinese People's War of Resistance Against Japanese Aggression and the World Anti-Fascist War" commemoration, as the end of World War II is known in China, I went to a special exhibition at the Museum of the War of Chinese People's Resistance Against Japanese Aggression in Beijing. It featured a display of Japanese wartime artifacts, including flags, under a glass floor. Chinese visitors were literally walking over Japan. "We want to keep Japan under our feet," Li Yake, a twenty-two-year-old college student doing a summer internship at the museum, told me.

At the same time as Xi began fuelling this anti-Japanese sentiment, Abe returned to power, hell-bent on achieving what he hadn't managed to during his first tenure as prime minister six years before: revise the pacifist constitution imposed on Japan by the American post-war occupiers.

Abe wants to free Japan of the restrictions that stipulate it must not maintain any "war potential" and can defend itself only if under attack. He is making progress, with a vote expected on amending the constitution this year, and is simultaneously seeking relatively small increases in Japan's defence budget. Of course, both moves are seen in Beijing as definitive proof of Japan's "re-militarisation."

In a visit to Tokyo in December, Steve Bannon, the arch-nationalist and erstwhile advisor to the American president, praised Abe for his efforts, calling him "Trump before Trump." Despite such words – meant as a compliment – and the rapport between Trump and Abe, there is deep anxiety among Japan's conservatives about the US commitment to the security alliance.

Abe was already worried about China's ascendancy when Trump started using Japan as an example of what was wrong with the United States' foreign policy. Why was the United States defending a rich country that was cutting the US's lunch when it came to trade? Trump's victory alarmed the Abe government, which had been sure of a Clinton win and had few contacts within the Trump camp. Senior officials told me that this was, in part, because they didn't want to risk Trump going out on the campaign trail claiming that the Japanese were begging to talk to him.

However, the Japanese prime minister has since skilfully handled Trump. Days after the 2016 election, Abe personally delivered a gold-plated golf driver to the president-elect in Trump Tower. On Trump's recent trip to Tokyo, Abe pandered to his counterpart's tastes, serving him hamburgers and steak, and taking him out on the golf course. Not a sliver of raw fish in sight.

Still, despite the public jollity, Japan's defence hawks are clearly worried. Now that North Korea has a demonstrated ability to send missiles to the mainland United States, will Washington – which is in the firing line – bother to defend its junior partner? Shigeru Ishiba, a hardline but nevertheless influential voice in the ruling Liberal Democratic Party, has stated that Japan should have the freedom to build nuclear weapons. Trump himself has several times said the same. Given Beijing wants nothing more than for the United States to leave the region, Trump's talk of closing American military bases in Japan and South Korea must have been music to Chinese ears.

But Xi has not capitalised on Trump's isolationist rhetoric to try to seduce Japan. Instead, he has stoked hostility towards its neighbour. McGregor's research underlines how much the foreign policy of both countries is driven by domestic considerations.

With Xi, Abe and Trump all set to enjoy several more years in power – not to mention Kim Jong-un in North Korea – these relationships will only become more toxic. That makes *Asia's Reckoning* crucial reading for our times.

Anna Fifield

Incorrigible Optimist: A Political Memoir
Gareth Evans
Melbourne University Press

Gareth Evans, foreign minister in the Hawke and Keating governments, talks a lot about the centrality of "good international citizenship" to his thinking on foreign policy. He defines this as a willingness to cooperate internationally to advance the public good. For Evans, prioritising "purposes beyond ourselves" – today, one might think of improving the international response to refugees, or nuclear weapons proliferation, or rising sea levels in the South Pacific – can be reconciled with hard-nosed arguments about the national interest. He not only regards the instinct for good international citizenship as a characteristic of the governments in which he served; he also understands it to be part of the Australian national psyche.

Evans' recent political memoir, *Incorrigible Optimist*, in which he lays out the key "ingredients" for effective foreign-policymaking in the Australian context, prompts a revisiting of the concept. His book covers his career in domestic politics, the international sphere and the higher education sector (he is now chancellor of the Australian National University). But throughout, the animating idea is good international citizenship. Today, when global politics are in flux, this raises several questions. What does it mean to be a good international citizen in 2018? More pointedly, can we realistically expect Australia to be one at such a challenging moment in history?

Evans, as he notes, was foreign minister at a "heady" time in history, from 1988 to 1996, when almost anything seemed possible. During this period, the Berlin Wall came down, the Cold War ended, Nelson Mandela was freed after twenty-seven years as a political prisoner (the book's cover features a photograph of the two of them) and apartheid was abolished in South Africa. It was the start of a "genuinely cooperative new era in international relations" and there was a "universal sense of optimism." (Not that Evans mentions this, but Bobby McFerrin's "Don't Worry, Be Happy" won song of the year at the 1989 Grammys.) This was enabled by a changing alignment of international interests, which provided the openings and opportunities for Evans' principled and ambitious style of active Australian diplomacy. His achievements included Australia's role in the Cambodian peace process – ending decades of violence – and in the international Chemical Weapons Convention. (The Asia-Pacific Economic Cooperation and the ASEAN Regional Forum, centred on regional cooperation,

were also conceived during the Hawke and Keating governments.)

We live, of course, in a very different world today, where uncertainty is the defining global sentiment. The "tectonic plates are shifting" and "power is moving from west to east," as Peter Varghese, former secretary of the Department of Foreign Affairs and Trade, put it. Donald Trump is tweeting from the White House, and the talk is about the need to protect Australian interests as China's ambitions grow and US power in the region declines.

Evans was a man "perfectly suited" to his times, Allan Gyngell, former director-general of the Office of National Assessments, observes in his book *Fear of Abandonment*. Evans' passion for the foreign-affairs portfolio lights up a sometimes dry memoir: "Bliss was it that dawn to be alive, but to be Foreign Minister was very heaven!" is his memorable opening to the chapter on diplomacy. Yet Evans' ideas about good international citizenship are as relevant as they ever were – particularly for Australia. They emphasise constructive relationship building; they focus on the bigger picture and eschew policy driven by short-term, selfish gains; they demand principles, and a willingness to stand up for those principles.

Foreign policy characterised by such positions is in the national interest, according to Evans, because it invites two hard-headed returns: it enhances a state's international reputation and it engenders reciprocity. This vision, with its defining commitment to multilateralism, is most often associated with Australian Labor governments and inspired by H.V. "Doc" Evatt's post–World War II legacy. But no country, no political party, has a monopoly on such behaviour, and most possess various attributes of the good international citizen. For example, the Labor government in which Evans was foreign minister continued to recognise Indonesia's occupation of East Timor. Similarly, the Howard government despised multilateralism and blindly followed the United States into the disastrous Iraq War in 2003 (which undermined the very "international institutions and rules" of which the Coalition's 2017 Foreign Policy White Paper makes so much). Yet Alexander Downer convinced John Howard to ratify the Rome Statute of the International Criminal Court.

It is difficult to reconcile Evans' belief that being a good international citizen is instinctive with a public that accepts the inhumane treatment of refugees on Manus Island and Nauru as the price for secure borders – policies pursued by both sides of politics. Could an Australian foreign minister prioritise "purposes beyond ourselves" and succeed (even survive) in 2018 as, the world over, countries turn inward, suspicion of the other grows and long-term liberal democracies appear unnervingly fragile? Yet Australia must.

What attributes, what vision, would an Australian foreign minister prioritising good international citizenship need today? For Evans, an effective foreign minister must, at a personal level, understand how to manage the politics of foreign policy – especially the relationship with the prime minister, but also with the cabinet, the party room, Parliament, interest groups and the media, as well as their own department and personal advisers. At a policy level, a commitment to good international citizenship includes following international law, believing in universal human rights and the role of the United Nations, investing in overseas aid programs and committing (indeed leading) internationalist solutions to world problems, whatever their nature.

The Turnbull/Bishop government is lacking in some of Evans' key ingredients. Julie Bishop is liked by her department; however, she is not regarded as a "conceptual thinker" of Evans' ilk. She has other constraints, including Australia's three-year terms, which are frustrating departmental efforts at long-term foreign-policy planning. In addition, Bishop heads a department whose resources have flatlined, and she oversees a decreased aid budget, where the folding of AusAID into DFAT has left staff concerned about the role aid now plays in Australian foreign policy. Australian money, for example, is poured into propping up an internationally condemned offshore immigration detention regime, and Australia, rather than supporting democratic principles in poor countries in the South Pacific, is benefiting from and entrenching weaknesses in the rule of law in those countries. Australia's relationships in South-East Asia – more crucial than ever, given concerns about China's ambitions, a point the White Paper recognises – are unbalanced: they are too security-focused and not altogether positive (particularly in relation to Indonesia). Meanwhile, Bishop sits in a cabinet where resources – and with them the power to make decisions that affect how Australia perceives itself and how it is perceived – are being sucked, disturbingly and without the public debate such a move warrants, into the new super Home Affairs portfolio, run by the duo known for their oversight of Australia's cruel refugee policies: Peter Dutton and Mike Pezzullo.

On the other hand, the Turnbull/Bishop government implicitly accepts some of the virtues of good international citizenship. Its White Paper preaches the need for openness – an "open society" at home, an "open, inclusive" region, an "open, outward-looking regional economy" – recognising that this is not a time for insular thinking. The government has also pursued multilateral engagement, winning a temporary seat on the UN Human

Rights Council. (How it reconciles this with its support of Myanmar's military, however, accused of perpetrating ongoing crimes against humanity against the minority Rohingya people, is difficult to follow.)

The benefits of good international citizenship in 2018 are clear; Australia's status as such a citizen is not. "Don't Worry, Be Happy" is no longer a song for our times, but some of Evans' ideas just may be.

Cynthia Banham

Blood and Silk: Power and Conflict in Modern Southeast Asia

Michael Vatikiotis
Weidenfeld & Nicolson

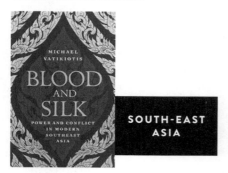

Every foreign correspondent, once they have spent a few years in a region, will be tempted to write a book about their experiences. This is always risky. Journalists may allow themselves to think they compose the first drafts of history, but the nature of their work usually gives them only a relatively superficial acquaintance with the issues they cover. The result may come across as too glib, too personal, too quickly overrun by events, more memoir than illuminating analysis.

Michael Vatikiotis calls on a lifetime of familiarity with South-East Asia to ask an impressive range of questions about how the region developed the political characteristics it has today and where it is heading. He has had the advantage of a more varied career than most foreign correspondents, which has moved from reporting to editing and, for more than a decade now, to conflict mediation. His book is far more than a journalist's memoir, although it cannot avoid some of the pitfalls of the genre.

The author was fortunate to arrive in South-East Asia long enough ago to have met some of the first generation of postcolonial nationalists, idealists and intellectuals with uplifting visions of what their countries could become. The contrast he paints between their dreams and the messy reality today is sobering.

Drawing on his experience as a private diplomat working for a Swiss-based mediation organisation, Vatikiotis examines the region's intractable conflicts – those that have held the border areas of so many countries in their grip for much of their postcolonial histories, and those, as in today's Thailand, that have flared up between rival political groups. These conflicts, he shows, have had a corrosive effect on the political culture but have been perpetuated by the shortsighted self-interest of entrenched elites.

The impressive economic progress in the region has, Vatikiotis argues, created spectacular levels of inequality of wealth and opportunity, which governments exploit to constrict the circle of power. Even the demands for change following the rapid adoption of social media have, he says, in one of many striking metaphors in the book, "fallen like spent bullets on the tough armour" of South-East Asia's overcentralised states. The author dwells on the many atrocities committed by state actors, for which there has rarely been redress. His experience in Indonesia often takes him back to the mass killings that accompanied the rise to power of General Suharto after 1965, which still cannot be discussed openly in the country. "Impunity afflicts the region like a chronic disease, one that leaves the host outwardly healthy but which nonetheless inhibits many critical bodily functions," he writes.

The gloomy prognosis seems apt for a book published at a time when the apparent democratic advances of the 1990s are being reversed in many countries or, in the case of Myanmar, accompanied by state-sponsored communal violence, and where the authoritarian model of China appears to be carrying more sway than the fading beacon of American democracy. Even in Indonesia, arguably the region's healthiest democracy, the author believes that the population, faced with a choice between divisive and corrupt politicians or formidable military leaders, "are not averse to a strong hand on the tiller – so long as it is cloaked in the trappings of democracy and not run by a thief."

Why, though, have democratic habits failed to take root in South-East Asia? Vatikiotis posits various reasons. He refers to the selfishness of elites, but it is hard to argue that Asian elites are any more innately selfish than their European, American or Australasian counterparts. He discusses the yearning for security in countries that have experienced debilitating instability; the instilled culture of patronage; and the weakness of historical analysis in societies that prefer "to interpret the past through comforting or heroic myth and legend, rather than by recording actual events," but none is explored sufficiently to provide any persuasive conclusion.

The absence of an independent and competent judiciary in almost all South-East Asian countries is touched on, but such an absence arguably poses the greatest obstacle to a more defiant democratic culture. Who can challenge holders of power if even the courts are in their pockets, as they so often are here? These days, those in authority resort to repressive laws, such as Malaysia's *Sedition Act* and Thailand's *Computer Crimes Act*, to silence dissent and intimidate the media (rather than outright thuggery and torture, as in the past). By contrast, in the United States we see President Trump's efforts to impose controversial measures being repeatedly and successfully challenged in the courts.

Likewise, South-East Asia's absence of an impartial civil service, with a sense of public duty as the prevailing ethic, deserves investigation. The riddle that anti-corruption campaigners in Asia confront is how to break the cycle of patronage and build genuinely independent institutions whose leaders cannot afford to be corrupted, where the shame and fear of legal retribution for bribery far outweighs any financial rewards. Singapore has done it, through the ruthless discipline of a determined state, and through generous salaries, which sap the incentive for corruption. But Singapore, a small city-state, is no model for the rest of South-East Asia.

Where Vatikiotis's analysis is strongest is, unsurprisingly, in the areas where he has most experience. The chapter on the growth of religious intolerance is superb. It chronicles the increasing appeal of piety among Indonesian student activists and the new urban middle class, the cynical exploitation of Islamic sensibilities by Malaysian political parties, and the rise of extremist jihadism, stirred by outside influences, as so many of the region's political movements have been.

His discussion of the lasting influence of colonial policies is likewise rewarding, although again demands further investigation. To what degree is the colonial practice of bringing in foreign workforces to Myanmar and Malaysia responsible for the racial tensions we see today? A large degree, surely, but were these explosive tensions inevitable? You will need to look elsewhere for more detailed answers.

Vatikiotis reveals his influences through his references to other thinkers, such as the British colonial official and anthropologist John Furnivall, who first coined the term "plural society" – although he meant unintegrated multi-ethnic communities rather than the more positive gloss the term has today. Or the Malaysian scholar Syed Hussein Alatas, who believed that colonial stereotypes of "the incompetent native" were adopted by the elites who ruled after independence. The text contains some lovely descriptive phrases, such as "the broad, seemingly unending tangle of family ties that provides the essential matting of Southeast Asian societies," which underscore the author's intimate familiarity with the region. There are also omissions – Vietnam, where presumably he has not spent much time, is barely mentioned.

On finishing *Blood and Silk*, I was left feeling it contained several potential books, with the author's years as a mediator, for example, opening a possible avenue to a more thorough work on border conflicts, or perhaps a detailed examination of the slow death of religious co-existence. For the newcomer to this extraordinary region, some persistence is required to follow the author's meandering recollections, spanning nearly forty years. For the old hand, and I count myself as one, there is much to learn from this book, opening many fresh paths of investigation.

This is at heart a compassionate but pessimistic reflection on the state of South-East Asia today, a stark rejoinder to the sunnier assessments of this being "Asia's century."

Jonathan Head

Australia's Northern Shield? Papua New Guinea and the Defence of Australia since 1880

Bruce Hunt
Monash University Publishing

It was an uncharacteristic misstep for Australia's usually impeccably shod foreign minister. As details spilt forth from the 2015 Budget night, interest was piqued by a small but controversial decision by Julie Bishop. Among the Department of Foreign Affairs and Trade's plans to set up five new diplomatic posts, funding had been allocated for the establishment of an Australian consular office on Bougainville, Papua New Guinea's rebellious, copper-rich island. The timing of this unheralded decision – accompanied by no explanation from Bishop – particularly intrigued those who followed events in PNG. Hovering for almost half a century with secessionist intent, riven by a civil war from 1988 to 1997, in which an estimated 15,000 to 20,000 people died, Bougainville, under the terms of a lengthy peace process, was poised to schedule a long-awaited referendum on independence. Now confirmed for June 2019, the referendum – which has generated less public interest or discussion in Australia than it should – could leave us with a new northern neighbour, or at worst trigger renewed violence after two decades of relative peace.

How to interpret the Commonwealth's decision to invest in a new diplomatic mission on a remote provincial island? While Bougainville once hosted one of the world's largest copper mines – Panguna, property of the Australian-owned Bougainville Copper – it now had scant commercial ties to Australia (unless you count Australia's generous and growing development assistance program on the island, which in 2017 reached A$50 million).

Canberra's apparent acquiescence to the inevitability of Bougainville's independence would represent a seismic shift in Australian's foreign policy. As Bruce Hunt reveals in meticulous detail in *Australia's Northern Shield?*, successive Australian cabinets have fretted over the possibility that our former colony would fragment upon independence. There were hours of cabinet discussion in 1975 about concerns that the country's 700 languages and deep tribal loyalties would ultimately prove stronger bonds than the freshly minted institutions of the young nation-state. It is an outcome that PNG thus far has managed, sometimes despite itself, to defy.

The morning after the budget, PNG's prime minister, Peter O'Neill, in Sydney for a speaking engagement, claimed he learnt of Bishop's decision to open a consulate in the Autonomous Region of Bougainville in the *Sydney Morning Herald*. O'Neill took instant and public umbrage. His foreign minister, Rimbank Pato, accused Canberra of being "outrageous" in undermining PNG's sovereignty, and "mischievous" for failing to inform the government of the plans – claims Bishop diplomatically but firmly denied. A short-lived ban on Australian tourists travelling to Bougainville was announced. Canberra, of course, had not jumped on the secessionist bandwagon. Despite DFAT's subsequent attempts to salvage the initiative, plans for the consular office were quietly shelved. O'Neill, wily, if unwise, had made his point.

Disappointingly, *Australia's Northern Shield?* does not address this curious incident, nor most of the past twenty-five years of a turbulent Australia–PNG relationship. Having twice headed DFAT's PNG Section, as well as serving as a diplomat with the Australian High Commission in Port Moresby and as a chief negotiator of the Bougainville peace process in 1999, Hunt would have vivid firsthand experience of the challenges of this modern relationship. The final chapter of this otherwise comprehensive book brings us only to the most recent renegotiation of a joint declaration of principles, in 2013. Nonetheless, Hunt, a research fellow at the Australian National University, has prowled through more than a century of records, including recently released cabinet notebooks that cover the period from the 1950s to the 1970s, to provide unique insight into the antecedents of the Australia–PNG relationship.

If PNG was once our northern shield, it still has potential to be our Achilles heel. Bougainville's struggles provide a perfect example. Indeed, Canberra's response has revealed as much about our own immaturity as a regional security leader as it has about the challenges of dealing with PNG.

Always the most recalcitrant of PNG's island provinces, Bougainville sits at the northernmost tip of the Solomon chain, the rest of which makes up the separate nation of Solomon Islands. Bougainvilleans originally insisted their province be called North Solomons, when PNG's disparate parts and peoples were being constructed into a nation-state. Force was first used in 1969 to put down a riot of Bougainvilleans resisting the relocation of their village, Rorovana, to make way for the bulldozers of Australian miners. Although the miners prevailed, the cognitive dissonance between Port Moresby and Arawa – the mining capital built on Rorovana land – was such that civil war broke out in 1988.

In the early days of the crisis, Canberra, lacking imagination or confidence or both, hid behind the excuse of non-intervention, failing to encourage or foster any mediation of the growing feud between Bougainville and Port Moresby. Yet we provided Iroquois helicopters to the unruly and embattled Papua New Guinea Defence Force (PNGDF), which promptly slung them with machine guns and turned them into gunships used at times to fire on villagers. It was a blatant breach of our human rights obligations, not seen so close to home till the more recent shame on Manus.

The fact that there was already so much violence by the

PNGDF towards Bougainvilleans, documented by myself and others, such as the ABC veteran Sean Dorney, made Canberra's decision to provide the Iroquois incomprehensible. As early as 1989 I can recall distraught parents demanding I accompany them to the Arawa morgue to witness the broken body of their teenage son, beaten with four-by-two planks by irate soldiers who claimed his dreads marked him as a member of the Bougainville Revolutionary Army.

It took until 1997 and then PNG prime minister Julius Chan's breathtakingly stupid decision to import South African mercenaries to put down the rebellion to finally bring everyone to their senses. The exposure of this scheme and the presence of these Sandline mercenaries on PNG territory was enough to force Chan from office and kick off a peace process that continues to this day, generously supported by Australian aid. Unsurprisingly, Canberra is not interested in seeing a return to hostilities. But we could find ourselves wedged in the post-referendum negotiations. Bougainville is clearly relying on Australia and New Zealand to support the expected breakaway vote, yet is already complaining that the "international community" is not being clear about its intentions. O'Neill and his cohorts in Port Moresby appear dangerously close to dishonouring the peace process and its lynchpin, the referendum, at the very least through a lack of proper resourcing. Meanwhile, the Autonomous Bougainville Government is struggling to get national support for even the preparation phases of the referendum.

As Hunt points out, Australia's 2016 Defence White Paper declared: "Australia cannot be secure if our immediate neighbourhood, including PNG, became the source of a threat to Australia." It would indeed be a paradox if our failure to understand and maintain an effective relationship with PNG proved to be the cause of such a threat. Through our development programs, Australia is doing pretty much all we can to support Bougainvilleans to conduct a free and fair process in 2019. Ironically but unsurprisingly, it is our relationship with Port Moresby, and the lack of influence we suffer, that could undermine our best intentions. With the referendum now just eighteen months away, Australian diplomats and aid workers alike will need to tread carefully to avoid future missteps.

Mary-Louise O'Callaghan

Straight Talk on Trade: Ideas for a Sane World Economy
Dani Rodrik
Princeton University Press

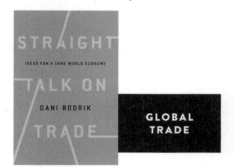

"**A**re economists responsible for Donald Trump's shocking victory in the US presidential election?" It hasn't exactly been the question on everyone's lips. But perhaps it should be.

This quote begins Dani Rodrik's new book, *Straight Talk on Trade*. A demolition of contemporary economic thought and, in particular, the unrelenting push for a globalised economy, it builds on Rodrick's previous work in challenging the dogmatic wisdom employed by most economists on everything from "free trade" to "structural reform."

What makes the study such a withering critique is that he employs orthodox methodology and theory to dismantle and dismiss widely accepted beliefs about our long-term economic goals and how to achieve them.

He also employs another powerful tool long abandoned by most practitioners of the dismal science: common sense.

Economics is supposed to be a study of human behaviour. Yet for a large part of the past half-century, humanity, with all its failings, has been gradually exorcised from the discipline. On this analysis, the boom and bust cycle, so prevalent in financial markets, was not due to irrational behaviour; instead, in the theoretical and unflinching world of modern economic thought, over-regulation, controls and red tape created inefficiencies and imbalances. Those who have argued for fairness – for balance between capital and labour – or who have warned of the political dangers associated with an inequitable distribution of wealth have found themselves under attack.

In recent years, China's transformation from third-world economic backwater to global industrial powerhouse only seemed to confirm the textbook argument that deregulation leads to a rising economic tide that lifts all boats. If removing some barriers had been so beneficial, why not get rid of them all? Or so the thinking evolved. Shades of grey were replaced by black and white in a world devoid of human foibles, where mathematical models, small government, deregulation and self-correcting markets ruled supreme.

Rodrik, Turkish-born and educated at Harvard and Princeton, has been one of the few dissenting voices – a role he has occupied for more than twenty years, starting with his 1997 tome, *Has Globalization Gone Too Far?* The political upheaval now coursing across the developed world – from Greece to Spain and Austria, to the United States, and to the United Kingdom's stunning decision to leave the European Union – appears to answer that question. So where has it all gone wrong?

According to Rodrik, the answer is simple. It was the downgrading of the nation-state, the local community, as world leaders rushed to embrace what he calls hyperglobalisation, convincing themselves that it was an unstoppable force. Rodrik argues that global growth is best facilitated by strong liberal democratic nation-states acting in the best interests of their constituents rather than submitting to a fundamentalist doctrine of international economic integration. The problem, as he explains it, is that while markets are global, governments are not. Which leaves only two remedies: limit the global nature of markets or extend the reach of governance.

In recent decades, the world has opted for the latter. But if we've learnt anything from the global financial crisis, it is that transnational regulation and governance remain weak. This has allowed corporations and financiers to trample over nation-states, often leaving a trail of wreckage in their path. (If a case study is required, one only needs to examine the grand European experiment: a single market and a single currency with a regional central bank, combined with national governments and fiscal policy. Economic integration without political integration.)

Our current dilemma is not new. As Rodrik points out, the first major push towards globalisation – from the late 1800s, when nations subjected themselves to the gold standard – ended in disaster, with the Great Depression and a political backlash that saw the rise of extreme political movements on the far right and left. It was the period after World War II, when the Bretton Woods Agreement put new controls on the free flow of capital, that global growth blossomed. And as Rodrik notes, China's phenomenal growth was not achieved through slavish devotion to free-market dogma, but through a carefully selected and managed approach to achieving social and economic goals.

So, what of the future? Rodrik argues the current backlash may be necessary to help avoid the same political upheaval and threat to freedom and democracy that followed the Great Depression – a political circuit-breaker rather than a retreat on trade. However, this analysis comes with a warning: "The appeal of populists is that they give voice to the anger of the excluded. They offer a grand narrative as well as concrete, if misleading and often dangerous, solutions," he writes.

Governments chose to allow the free flow of global capital. They allowed it to continue even after the global financial crisis. Rodrik argues that bold measures now are required to restrict these flows so that communities can reclaim control of their economic future. While it is an argument that until recently has been akin to economic heresy, Rodrik insists it is necessary for the survival of capitalism and free-market economies:

> If one lesson of history is the danger of globalization running amok, another is the malleability of capitalism. It was the New Deal, the welfare state, and controlled globalization ... that eventually

gave market-oriented societies a new lease on life and produced the postwar boom. It was not tinkering and minor modification of existing policies that produced these achievements but rather radical institutional engineering.

For Rodrik, it's time for economists to be less dogmatic and to point out the pitfalls and dangers of policies – rather than simply barrelling blindly down the path of least resistance, otherwise known as conventional wisdom.

Ian Verrender

The Army and the Indonesian Genocide: Mechanics of Mass Murder
Jess Melvin
Routledge

I t has been the mystery of a lifetime. What really happened in Indonesia in the early hours of 1 October 1965 and the months that followed? It started with rebel troops seizing the centre of Jakarta, then an

army countermove. By the time I first went backpacking across the archipelago, five years later, it was all over: the revolutionary president Sukarno out of power, the once-triumphant Partai Komunis Indonesia obliterated, a stolid pro-Western general named Suharto the new president.

Western governments accepted the version put out by Suharto. The PKI had lunged for power, using sympathetic officers led by a Lieutenant-Colonel Untung to seize the top army generals, allegedly because these high-living, pro-American officers were about to overthrow Sukarno. The rebels drove them to a communist training camp at Lubang Buaya (Crocodile Hole), where the prisoners were tortured, sexually mutilated and executed before a crowd of frenzied PKI members. But the obscure Suharto had quickly rallied loyal troops.

Over the following weeks, a wave of killing erupted, as ordinary people turned on PKI supporters in revulsion at the party's "coup attempt." It was all "spontaneous." Estimates of the dead went as high as two million, but the smashing of the largest communist party outside the Soviet Union and China was worth it for Washington, London and Canberra. It was "the West's best news for years in Asia," said *Time* magazine. "With 500,000 to one million sympathisers knocked off," said Australian prime minister Harold Holt, "I think it is safe to assume a reorientation has taken place."

When I returned to Jakarta as a freelance correspondent in January 1975, it was starting to look a bit embarrassing. Suharto had shown his authoritarian colours by crushing anti-corruption protests and arresting many of the liberals who'd helped him come to power. The dead were invisible, but hundreds of thousands of PKI members and alleged sympathisers were still in camps.

In 1976, we foreign journalists were invited to watch a group of low-level prisoners, young men and women with serious, careworn faces, take oaths of allegiance to Indonesia before being released after a decade of imprisonment without trial. At the end of 1977, we were flown to the island of Buru, landing on a former Japanese airfield marked with craters from Allied bombing in World War II. A launch took us on a Conradian journey upriver to a settlement of barracks and dry fields, where suspect intellectuals were held for re-education in Suharto's New Order. Men with the ragged appearance of peasants turned out to be publishers, journalists and academics. The novelist Pramoedya Ananta Toer showed me the corner cubicle in his barracks where he was allowed to write. In the coming two years, nearly all of Buru's prisoners were released, although kept under constant surveillance. A few decided to remain. The local crocodile population, once decimated by the starving prisoners, has returned.

Foreign scholars had meanwhile started questioning the creation myth of the New Order. The rebel colonel Untung had been one of Suharto's commandos parachuted into Dutch New Guinea in 1962. Suharto had attended his wedding. And why was Suharto left off the abduction list? Some readily named Suharto as the *dalang* (puppet-master). Yet the PKI's general secretary, Dipa Nusantara Aidit, was in close touch with Untung, through his secret agent "Sjam." Why did this pair fire up Untung to act? Did they discover a genuine plot among the generals? Or was Sjam a double agent?

Recent work by scholars John Roosa and Taomo Zhou in US and Chinese diplomatic archives show the army and the PKI each waiting for the other to strike first. Untung gave the army its excuse. As Australian scholar Jess Melvin notes in this elegantly written new book, based on her prize-winning doctoral thesis: "It is hard to imagine the military could have come up with a more perfect sequence of events if it had tried."

Melvin doesn't reveal the innermost mystery of 1 October 1965. But through 3000 pages of top-secret documents she found while researching in post-tsunami Aceh, she has exposed the army's plotting before, during and after the Untung move. Her trove includes

the year-end report for 1965 by the Aceh region military commander, Brigadier General Ishak Djuarsa. It details how civilian death squads were formed ahead of 1 October and launched soon afterwards against Aceh's PKI rank and file and Beijing-aligned ethnic Chinese. Djuarsa was acting on orders passed down the army command to "exterminate to the roots" the communist base. It is a powerful addition to our knowledge about the 1965–66 events.

By year's end, Djuarsa reported 1941 cases of public killings to army headquarters. Soldiers carried out many of the killings, though Melvin writes that "the actual act of killing would be delegated as far down the chain of command as possible." Djuarsa, touring Aceh's towns from 7 October, stirred civilians, telling them that if they did not participate in the killings, they could expect to be punished or even killed themselves. He reported that, after hearing him speak in town squares, "the people of Aceh straight away moved to exterminate the PKI."

Melvin has also collected harrowing accounts from survivors and perpetrators. In Takengon, in the coffee-growing highlands, PKI suspects were confined in local halls, then taken out at night, sacks over their heads and hands bound, to isolated sites, where they were shot or slashed, their bodies pushed down the mountainside. A witness named Kadir saw the execution of Sambami, the wife of a doctor, who was shot clutching her newborn: "The bullet passed through the body of the child and then into Sambami. They died together, Sambami screaming for her child." As for the perpetrators Melvin interviewed, "their greatest regret was that they had not received more recognition for their actions." Melvin's documentation destroys the argument that the killings were beyond the control of the army, or were at all spontaneous.

A central question arising from the book is: how typical was Aceh? Melvin shows convincingly that the army called the shots throughout. Because of the army's frontline status in Sukarno's "Crush Malaysia" campaign, and the PKI's local passivity, military commanders were able to put plans into operation as soon as Suharto telegrammed news of the Untung "coup" on 1 October. Elsewhere in Indonesia, similar operations had differing timelines. In Central Java, Suharto had first to quell garrisons that came out for Untung by sending in the army's RPKAD special forces (now known as Kopassus). These commandos then instructed local Muslim, Christian and nationalist organisations on how to carry out mass killings. In late 1965 and early 1966, this built into an outbreak of mass murder that choked rivers and filled ravines with bodies, extending to East Java and Bali.

Another question hangs over the use of the word "genocide" for the killings. The 1965–66 army operation aimed to "exterminate to the roots," and Melvin argues that the designation of the PKI as "atheist" makes it a protected religious group under the 1948 convention – and Indonesia's complicity subject to international criminal jurisdiction. She is not alone in applying the term. On the fiftieth anniversary of Untung's putsch, former Australian foreign minister Gareth Evans called the slaughter "the least studied and least talked-about political genocide of the last century."

As this grim anniversary approached, I was back in Indonesia, and it appeared the nation was at last starting to talk about it. Survivor groups were agitating for redress. A mayor in Sulawesi erected a memorial at a local killing site. The magazine *Tempo* published a book-length report; scholars such as Baskara T. Wardaya detailed accounts of mass killings, torture, imprisonment and rape; Joshua Oppenheimer's award-winning documentary *The Act of Killing* was widely viewed.

The new president, Joko Widodo, promised a full inquiry, and in April 2016 his government sponsored a "National Symposium on the 1965 Tragedy." However, his top security minister, Luhut Panjaitan, a former Kopassus general, disputed that large numbers were killed and asked where the mass graves were to prove it. A claque of retired generals and Muslim hotheads protested against further inquiries outside the presidential palace.

Today, activists trying to excavate suspected gravesites are still harried by local security agents. Ultranationalist *preman* (vigilantes) break up PKI survivor meetings. Army commanders and Muslim groups declare communism is somehow still a threat in consumerist Indonesia. As president, Widodo attends the annual commemoration at the Crocodile Hole, where the museum still shows schoolchildren the army's false story of 1 October. Suharto's New Order is still alive.

The term "genocide" can get backs up rather than encourage openness. Melvin thinks Washington, London and Canberra "have been able to escape scrutiny for their own roles in this atrocity" and should open their intelligence files on the events. "It is farcical to believe the Indonesian state will spontaneously initiate a meaningful truth-seeking, let alone justice-seeking, investigation into these dark events without serious pressure being applied," she writes. She is right: for now, the truth only trickles out and the record further darkens.

Hamish McDonald

Correction: In Issue 1's interviews with Paul Keating, three questions were wrongly attributed. The first three questions attributed to Michael Fullilove were asked by Allan Gyngell (p. 15) and Nick Bisley (pp. 16–17).

Correspondence

"Mugged by Sentiment"
by James Curran

Rory Medcalf

ustralian Foreign Affairs has taken on a tough task. It offers a distinctly Australian platform for timely, in-depth and original analysis about the challenges and opportunities in the difficult international environment ahead.

An independent foreign policy is what any self-respecting country needs. But it can only be as effective as the ideas for action that go with it. The first tranche of essays, however articulate, could have gone further to explain in practical terms what is to be done.

Certainly there's lots of engaging assessment and commentary from some leading names in the national debate. In places, I found myself in furious agreement, notably with Allan Gyngell's recognition that the call for an "independent Australian foreign policy" is "the wrong way of looking at it" – after all, such calls "deflect responsibility for our own actions." It is not independence our external engagement needs – we have that already – but rather "substance, subtlety and creativity."

In other places, the assertions on offer raised as many questions as they answered – arguably part of the purpose of the publication.

James Curran's historical research on the US–Australia alliance is renowned and his essay "Mugged by Sentiment" (issue 1, October 2017) highly readable, but the piece does not prove his assertion that the hallmarks of current alliance policy are sentimentalism and complacency. The 2017 Foreign Policy White Paper can be read in many ways, but this is not one of them; not if studied in its totality. It is easy to find examples of politicians trumpeting an appeal to the past – notably Prime Minister Turnbull's remarks at the commemorations on the floating museum USS *Intrepid* – but it is unusual for a historian of Curran's calibre to conclude that what politicians say is what they think. Some senior figures may profess to buy the idea that America will forever be by our side because of what we have done together in the past. But on the whole, Australian policy is informed much more deeply by pragmatism.

That said, I agree with Curran's conclusion that the alliance with the United States has proved its resilience before and will survive the Trump presidency. It would have been useful if he had also mentioned the economic pillars of the relationship, including levels of US investment in Australia that in recent times have grown more in one year than the entire stock of Chinese investment here.

Rory Medcalf, head of the National Security College,
Australian National University

Richard Menhinick

n his essay "Mugged by Sentiment" (issue 1, October 2017), James Curran has summarised significant issues for the US–Australia relationship, including the role of sentimentalism in Australian reactions to the forty-fifth president of the United States. While focusing predominantly on difference in attitudes in Australia to the alliance, he also wrote that "the idea that the passing of Trump from the scene will remove the toxicity from American politics is surely a fantasy." This included a mention of American exceptionalism and forces within America.

In my view, this is the overriding issue, not Trump himself, as the emergence of such a person as president reflects worrying societal beliefs and divisions in America. These may place more strain on Australia's alliance with the United States than anything else.

During my three years living in the States, where I most recently worked at the US Central Command headquarters in Florida, it became apparent to me that Australians do not grasp that the existential alliance problem is that our great military ally is very different to us, not just in accent, population or economic weight, but also in attitudes that underpin society and policy. This is dangerous, as it provides Australian politicians the ability to resort to sentimentalism, as James Curran summarises so well, while ignoring forces that shape America.

Americans and Australians tend to have very different attitudes to the role of government. In America government intervention is largely unwelcome, whereas attempts to improve society and reduce inequity in Australia are due mainly to strong societal expectations of government. This view is not always efficient or effective, but it underpins a more inclusive society. While Americans pride themselves in being ferociously independent of government, they are also extremely patriotic. The mantra of President Donald Trump is to "make America great again." His approach may be truculent, but his dogmas reflect mainstream America. Life is defined through individual freedom and success. Government intervention is seen as a sign of weakness, decline and a culture of entitlement. The approach to guns is similarly driven by individual rights trumping the collective good.

The United States has protected the free world, but all too often sits outside international agreements and norms. It is difficult to deliver an equitable foreign policy if domestic societal beliefs prevent it. Therefore, it should come as no surprise that the United States, not just Trump, finds it increasingly difficult to compromise internationally. Americans have difficulty recognising that other countries have their own areas of interest and legitimate concerns. There is a profound lack of interest in how other nations do things. This is the significant challenge for the alliance.

The US and international commentators focus predominantly on Trump, his policies and statements. However, Trump was voted in because what he said reflected the sentiments of millions of Americans. He is not the most extreme elected politician in the nation: the views of many senators and members of Congress from the Republican Party, not only Trump, should reverberate as chilling to Australia, despite our sentimentalism.

Belief in US exceptionalism is existential to American society, views and interactions with the world. This is a constant, even if the nature and limits of American power changes. Experience shows that the US military and political elite treasure their friends when they do what the United States wants. Their view of their national interests, from their own rules-based perspective, drives everything. James Curran talks of the dangers of Australian support being taken for granted by the United States. My view is that due to thirty-plus years of deficient defence spending, we are already there.

In twenty-first-century America, disunity, exclusion and anger triumph over unity and inclusion. This is the key issue for the alliance in the coming years, not Trump. Unhappily, Australia does not comprehend this.

Richard Menhinick, retired senior officer
of the Royal Australian Navy

James Curran responds

irst things first: Rory Medcalf well knows that my article was drafted before the release of the 2017 Foreign Policy White Paper. That document eschews sentiment in its treatment of Canberra's relationship with Washington. Indeed, nowhere in it does the word "primacy" accompany the name "America." White Papers, though, tend to ward off bouts of mellifluence. So it remains the case that the prevailing political response in Canberra to this American president has been one primarily driven by the remembrance of things past: a time before Trump. The evidence for this is overwhelming, but equally such a posture is not a surprise: shocks such as Trump often prompt a retreat to cosier rhetorical havens. In my article, I point out both the shortcomings and the potential benefits of this approach where this particular US leader is concerned.

Speaking at the launch of the White Paper, the Minister for Foreign Affairs, Julie Bishop, gave renewed voice to sentimentalism and complacency by stating her absolute confidence in the enduring hegemonic role that the United States would play in Asia. The point is this: senior figures in the government and the more hawkish among Canberra's national security community continue to understand American power through an older Cold War (or, at best, a post–Cold War) prism. They will not easily let go of the United States with which they became so familiar: the America of Kennedy, Reagan, Bush Snr and Clinton. It is surely not necessary here to underline the importance of understanding the intellectual history and worldview that leaders bring to office. Medcalf instead trots out the familiar line about the prevalence of "pragmatism" in alliance policy – a convenient ruse to downplay the role of history and culture in shaping Australia's approach to the world.

Medcalf then damns me with faint praise by saying that a historian of my credibility could hardly fail to appreciate the difference between what politicians "say" and what they "think." In essence, he finds fault with the fact that I take political language seriously. Medcalf implies that we should simply ignore what politicians say. Rhetoric, according to him, is but a superficial gloss. Only the "insiders," therefore, those supposedly privy to the inner councils of government, can truly divine the substance of politics.

Why, then, are the speeches of leaders still relentlessly scrutinised for what they reveal about the contours and content of government policy? The short answer is that for all the tweeting of the times, speeches still matter. Language matters. And so does sustained, reasoned argument. As the American historian Michael Hunt has argued, rhetoric should be studied for "both the deep-seated attitudes it reveals and the action it may portend." Philip Williamson, biographer of British prime minister Stanley Baldwin, put it even more succinctly: "Politicians are what they speak and publish."

Was not Malcolm Turnbull's statement last year that Australia was "joined at the hip" with Washington over North Korea a fusion of statement and thought? Can Medcalf really sail breezily past the policies that flowed from Harold Holt's declaration that he was "all the way with LBJ," Hawke's and Keating's language of "engagement" with Asia, or John Howard's dictum that Australia didn't need to choose between its history and geography? These statements had real policy consequences. If Medcalf undertook a close study of the foreign-policy statements and utterances of many recent prime ministers, he may well find that there is not always so vast a gulf between what politicians say and what they think.

Medcalf's response is emblematic of a particular genre of foreign-affairs analysis: captive of the present moment, loathe to look to the past and prone to missing the tectonic forces moving beneath the surface of events.

Richard Menhinick's argument, on the other hand, cuts to the very core of the issue: namely, the importance of understanding American exceptionalism and how the deeper social and cultural forces roiling US politics are undermining, if not shattering, any public approval for an ambitious foreign policy. Menhinick's prognosis as to where Australia sits in the American pantheon will disturb alliance true believers, but it is undoubtedly much closer to the mark than the rather tired recitals from leaders on both sides of the Pacific that the relationship is "stronger than ever."

Australia continues to gain great benefits from its relationship with the United States. But any alliance has to adjust to changing circumstances and, occasionally, free itself from the comforting nostrums of old.

James Curran, professor of modern history, University of Sydney;
non-resident fellow, the Lowy Institute

"The Changing Face of Australia"
by George Megalogenis

Jieh-Yung Lo

George Megalogenis's article "The Changing Face of Australia" (issue 1, October 2017) spoke to me like no other. His article validates the potential of those from culturally diverse backgrounds – like myself, an Australian-born Chinese – and the role we can play to advance Australia's interests regionally and globally.

Megalogenis points out that Australia's foreign policy remains deeply rooted in an Anglo past. This is because the relevant policymakers and the federal parliament do not reflect the cultural, ethnic and linguistic diversity of Australia. Research published last year by the Australian Human Rights Commission found that 95 per cent of parliamentarians are of Anglo-Celtic-European heritage. Chinese and Indian Australians, the two communities Megalogenis mentioned in his article, do not hold a single seat in federal parliament. If parliament is a reflection of the face of modern Australia, there should be at least 104 MPs from culturally diverse backgrounds.

Megalogenis is correct to point out that Australian businesses happily trade with Asia, but the doors remain firmly shut for Asian-Australians in executive boardrooms. Even though 9 per cent of the Australian labour force has an Asian cultural heritage, only 2 per cent of executives in ASX200 companies have Asian cultural origins.

In the Australian public service, 98 per cent of federal and state secretaries and heads of departments come from an Anglo-Celtic-European background. Just 5 per cent of public service employees identified as being from a non–English speaking/culturally diverse background in 2012–13. These figures suggest barriers within the public service that are preventing it from attracting, retaining and promoting talent from diverse backgrounds.

To complete the transition to a Eurasian nation as proposed by Megalogenis, Australia needs to actively engage with and involve its growing culturally diverse communities in foreign-policy creation and implementation. Australians from culturally diverse backgrounds, as citizens passionate about Australia's role and place in the world, have much to offer.

In the 2017 Foreign Policy White Paper, the federal government committed to working with Australia's diasporas and culturally diverse communities. The paper states that "these communities often have the connections, language skills and cultural understanding to assist Australia to deepen ties with other countries." As Megalogenis said: "Every migrant is a potential emissary. Welcome them, and their mother country will view Australia more favourably. Alienate them, and their mother country will be less inclined to do us a favour."

From my experience engaging in cultural diplomacy – establishing a successful sister/friendship relationship between the cities of Xi'an and Hobart – I believe this is Australia's competitive edge. My knowledge of both languages, cultures, history, legal and political systems, and my appreciation for China–Australia relations, enabled the initial establishment of the relationship, which, after visits from various delegations, developed into mutual trust, respect and good-will. The decision to work with Xi'an and Hobart opened a new frontier for China–Australia relations as the focus moved beyond the major cities into new regions and opportunities for both countries. Given the chance, culturally diverse Australians can be emissaries who change the way Australia engages with the region and the world.

Moving forward, the Department of Foreign Affairs and Trade (DFAT) should expand its Agency Multicultural Plan to inform culturally diverse communities of Australia's foreign-policy objectives. In addition to strengthening language and cultural capabilities within the department, DFAT should seek to employ more culturally diverse Australians and train them to undertake diplomatic missions, strengthen people-to-people links and represent Australia's interests aboard.

There are only a few nations on earth that possess such rich cultural diversity. It is our foreign-policy edge. Policymakers should be harnessing our skills, abilities and knowledge as we attempt to build closer relationships with regional and global neighbours. It is difficult to predict when Australia will successfully complete its transition to a Eurasian nation. But when our public and private institutions and their senior leadership reflect the cultural, ethnic and linguistic diversity of Australia, I'd say we're halfway there. And having a future prime minister from a background other than Anglo-Celtic-European would definitely complete our transition.

Jieh-Yung Lo, writer and policy adviser

John Fitzgerald

n contrast to earlier generations of migrants, many of today's newcomers acquire Australian citizenship through business visas or by entering under temporary work visa programs, or by forking out hefty sums for university degrees. These arrivals could hardly be faulted for regarding citizenship as a market transaction rather than a civic commitment. To date, though, there is little evidence that this is the case. Still, if the country they left behind were to regard them as absentee compatriots or as an extension of its interests abroad, recent cohorts of Australian citizens could find themselves in an invidious position. On the one hand, they could be subjected to appeals to "homeland" patriotism. On the other, they could fall under suspicion in Australia as potential risks to national cohesion, sovereignty and security.

George Megalogenis's insightful essay, "The Changing Face of Australia" (issue 1, October 2017), alludes to this dilemma in tracing major changes to Australia's immigration intake. New arrivals are younger, more highly skilled and better educated, and arrive in greater numbers than ever before from India and China. Unlike their predecessors, they do not take two or more generations to make good but arrive cashed up, confident and ready to do business. Is Australia ready for them?

Megalogenis names some of the challenges this shifting immigrant profile presents for Australia in a rapidly evolving strategic environment. In the case of China, earlier cohorts owed their livelihood and identity to their adopted country, Australia. More recent immigrants derive their wealth, power and identity from China, and Beijing is not inclined to let them forget it.

Megalogenis argues that for the first time in our history an immigrant community is living under the "watchful eye" of a foreign government that regards them as an extension of itself within Australia. He presents a "call to arms" to Australian governments "to elevate migration to a first-order concern for foreign affairs" – not just to get migration right but to navigate an independent foreign policy beholden neither to the United States nor to China.

The question the essay raises for me is whether Megalogenis's call to arms on foreign policy needs to be balanced by an equally strident call to arms on multicultural policy. Are multicultural policies and programs keeping pace with these developments? In particular, do earlier assumptions around multicultural media still hold up?

SBS Radio exemplifies an earlier model of analogue multiculturalism. Its programming is multicultural in the aggregate and monocultural in the case of each unique listener. It offers Arabic one moment, Tagalog another and Cantonese the next. The imagined community of SBS Radio corresponds to no particular citizen but at least everyone gets a guernsey. It's fair – and it's largely redundant.

The global reach of social media and digital communications based outside Australia is placing analogue multiculturalism under stress. Indian-Australian communities can tune in digitally to more than 100 television and radio platforms in Hindi, twenty-four hours a day, and to dozens more in their local languages transmitted directly from India. Chinese-Australian communities can do the same with Mandarin programming, including access to local radio stations operated on behalf of the Central Propaganda Bureau of the Chinese Communist Party (CCP). Why would active young professional Chinese Australians await their turn on the SBS queue when they can download news or gossip on webchat any time, or tune in to Tommy Jiang's local Chinese radio network over breakfast, broadcasting Beijing propaganda any time of day?

It is time Australian businesses and governments started investing disproportionately in servicing rapidly growing twenty-first-century immigrant communities, particularly Chinese and Indian communities. One idea worthy of consideration is the provision of twenty-four-hour radio and digital-media coverage in Mandarin and Hindi. The aim of these platforms would be to welcome new arrivals as Australians in their own languages, on the SBS model, and to encourage their participation in Australian civic life. Tweaking multicultural media policy in this way could mark one step towards converting citizenship from a market transaction into a civic commitment by playing the loyalty game "on our own terms," as Megalogenis advises.

A second challenge lies with the mainstream Australian media. China's ambassador to Australia recently claimed that the Australian media has "unscrupulously vilified" the country's Chinese communities and "tarnished Australia's reputation as a multicultural society." The ambassador's claim is baseless insofar as it relates to media coverage of CCP interference in Australia, which touches legitimately on issues of national sovereignty. China's ambassador is on firmer ground if he is referring to media coverage of real-estate and land investments. Coverage of these issues often focuses on Chinese-Australian residents and citizens, or on Chinese business firms, where the primary objection raised is that the investors are "Chinese." This is arguably discriminatory and risks tarnishing Australia's reputation as a multicultural society.

There is a world of difference between shock-jock journalism of this kind and coverage of CCP infiltration of Australian institutions such as political parties, media companies, universities and community organisations. Obscuring the difference by claiming that all criticism of China's activities in Australia is overblown or racially charged does not help. Some is, and some is not. The mainstream media need to get this right.

John Fitzgerald, professor emeritus, Centre for Social Impact,
Swinburne University of Technology

The Back Page

THE MUNICH ANALOGY

What is it: A comparison of any act of diplomacy to Neville Chamberlain's "appeasement" of Hitler at the Munich Conference in 1938.

Who buys it: Many pundits, particularly American conservatives, who have used it for every president since Truman who tries to compromise. Reagan, Bush Snr, Clinton and especially Obama have all been analogised. Bill Kristol (founder, *The Weekly Standard*) has been "reminded" of Hitler and Churchill on more than sixty occasions.

Who doesn't: Tom Shachtman (writer, *Foreign Policy*) called it an "uber-analogy" that "needs to go." As early as 1965, George Kennan (diplomat, USA) told a Senate committee, "I think that no episode, perhaps, in modern history has been more misleading than the Munich Conference."

Peak Munich: Probably the Iran nuclear deal, where everyone from Bret Stephens (columnist, *New York Times*) to Benjamin Netanyahu (prime minister, Israel) used it. Allen West (former congressman, USA) compared Obama to Chamberlain *and* Hitler.

Comments: Unlike European powers, America had little experience with bitter diplomatic concession, at least before Vietnam. Presidents gestated the analogy: John F. Kennedy wrote his Harvard thesis on "appeasement at Munich"; Lyndon Johnson said during Vietnam, "I wasn't any Chamberlain umbrella man" (Chamberlain famously toted his brolly post-conference); and Richard Nixon was so obsessed with being analogised that he forbade staff meeting him at airports from carrying umbrellas.

The last word: "Appeasement in itself may be good or bad according to the circumstances. Appeasement from weakness and fear is alike futile and fatal. Appeasement from strength is magnanimous and noble, and might be the surest and perhaps the only path to world peace." Winston Churchill (statesman, Britain).